Online Predators

Melissa Abramovitz

ReferencePoint Press®

San Diego, CA

About the Author
Melissa Abramovitz is an award-winning author who has published hundreds of nonfiction maga-
zine articles and more than fifty educational books for children and teens, along with short stories,
poems, picture books, and a book for writers. Melissa graduated from the University of California–
San Diego with a degree in psychology and is also a graduate of the Institute of Children's Literature.

© 2017 ReferencePoint Press, Inc.
Printed in the United States

For more information, contact:
ReferencePoint Press, Inc.
PO Box 27779
San Diego, CA 92198
www. ReferencePointPress.com

LIBRARY OF CONGRESS CATALOGING-IN-PUBLICATION DATA

Names: Abramovitz, Melissa, 1954- author.
Title: Online predators / by Melissa Abramovitz.
Description: San Diego, CA : ReferencePoint Press, 2017. | Series: Digital
  issues | Audience: Grade 9 to 13. | Includes bibliographical references and index.
Identifiers: LCCN 2016021581 (print) | LCCN 2016028612 (ebook) | ISBN
  9781682820926 (hardback) | ISBN 9781682820933 (eBook)
Subjects: LCSH: Internet--Safety measures--Juvenile literature. | Internet
  and children--Juvenile literature. | Privacy, Right of--Juvenile
  literature. | Cyberbullying--Juvenile literature.
Classification: LCC HQ784.I58 A27 2016 (print) | LCC HQ784.I58 (ebook) | DDC
  004.67/8083--dc23
LC record available at https://lccn.loc.gov/2016021581

CONTENTS

The Dark Side of the Internet

The Internet has given people unprecedented opportunities to communicate, find information, express opinions, shop, and enjoy games, movies, and music. However, many people have corrupted this freely accessible connectivity by using it for nefarious purposes. Such people are known as online predators, cyberpredators, or informally as "trolls."

The online Merriam-Webster dictionary defines a *predator* as "a person who looks for other people in order to use, control, or harm them in some way." This definition is derived from the general definition of a predator, which is "an animal that lives by killing and eating other animals; an animal that preys on other animals."[1] Although different predators operate in different ways, all of them—including online predators—use stealth to subjugate and harm others for their own purposes.

The Internet makes stealth easier than it has ever been. Cybercriminals hide behind fake names and locations and operate across long distances, which makes it difficult for law enforcement agencies to find and arrest them. Joseph M. Demarest, assistant director of the FBI's Cyber Division, told a US Senate committee in 2014 that whereas criminals "were previously confined by time, distance, and physical location," cybercriminals are "launching attacks from all over the world at literally the speed of light."[2]

The Proliferation of Cyberpredators

The number of predators and victims has grown tremendously since the Internet became operational in the mid-1990s. Each year millions of online crimes affect millions of victims emotionally, physically, financially, and socially. Predators' methods of perpetrating cybercrimes also expand as technologies evolve, and many cybercriminals commit an increasing range of crimes as well. Sexual or financial predators may also be cyberbullies, stalkers, identity thieves, and blackmailers, which compounds the challenges faced by police and victims' advocacy organizations who work to stop these criminals.

One reason for the rapid proliferation of cyberpredators and victims is that the number of Internet-connected people has grown tremendously. Indeed, it is difficult to think of a technological innovation that has spread more rapidly and more widely than the Internet. In one of the most intense periods of growth, for example, the number of Internet users increased from 350 million in 2000 to more than 2 billion by 2010. Continuing expansion has made more and more people vulnerable to online predators. In addition, the increase in smartphone use has augmented the number of people continuously online. Those who use social media, messaging, shopping, banking, and other apps around the clock are often unaware that these activities make them more vulnerable to predators.

> "The tools and techniques developed by cybercriminals are increasing in sophistication at an incredible rate."[3]
>
> —National security experts Kristin Finklea and Catherine A. Theohary.

An Ongoing Battle

Keeping up with cyberpredators and their new methods is a full-time job for many law enforcement and cybersecurity experts. As fast as new security barriers and sleuthing techniques are adopted, criminals invent new ways to hide, hack, and harass, often staying one step ahead of authorities. According to a 2015 report by national security experts Kristin Finklea and Catherine A. Theohary, "The tools and techniques developed by cybercriminals are increasing in sophistication at an incredible rate."[3]

The fact that cyberattacks can be directed at government and institutional computer systems as well as at individuals further enhances these challenges. Hackers motivated by political or religious issues, greed, or simply a desire to make trouble have already shut down or done significant harm to financial institutions, multinational corporations, and even entire countries. In 2007, for instance, the Estonian government and economy shut down after Russian protesters flooded government, banking, and communications websites with cybertraffic, resulting in what is known as a distributed denial of service. Security experts worry that since most power grids, air traffic control, and military weapons systems are controlled by computers, cyberpredators could use similar tactics to trigger international crises of immense proportions.

Does the Internet Create Predators?

The range and proliferation of online crimes have led to debates about whether the Internet and digital devices *create* criminals or merely provide convenient operating methods for established criminals to use. Evidence supports both contentions.

University of California–Los Angeles neuroscientist Gary Small, for instance, believes that excessive use of digital technologies, exposure to violent video games and movies, and a lack of in-person interactions negatively affect brain development in children and teenagers. Small's research has shown that when people's brains become "wired" to multitask and flip from one violent or disturbing game, news story, or social media bashing event to another, there are grave consequences. "Many people are desensitizing their neural circuits to the horrors they see, while not getting much, if any, off-line training in empathetic skills,"[4] he says. This results in a person's brain creating fewer of the neural connections that underlie feelings of compassion and empathy, and Small believes such individuals are more likely to become cyberpredators. Other researchers have supported these findings with work that shows that online anonymity can push people who would not commit crimes offline to do so in cyberspace. This is known as online disinhibition.

On the other hand, researchers at California State University–Dominguez Hills have found that, in general, spending time online does not affect college students' ability to feel empathy and interact with others. Research by psychology professor Azy Barak at the University of Haifa in Israel also indicates that online disinhibition can lead to negative *or* positive behaviors, depending on the individual. People who are naturally shy or reluctant to share their feelings may participate in online support groups because of what psychologists call "benign disinhibition." On the other hand, those who hide their abusive personalities offline may become cyberpredators because of "toxic disinhibition." As Barak writes, "Many

Some experts contend that constant exposure to violent video games and movies negatively affects brain development. Lack of in-person interactions compounds the problem.

people, when immersed in cyberspace, remove their offline masks and expose their more authentic selves."[5]

Thus, research has not really answered the question of whether the Internet turns people into cyberpredators or whether such predators have just found a new criminal outlet. But either way, scientists agree that digital technologies and the Internet are not inherently evil. Many would agree with what technology experts Eric Schmidt and Jared Cohen say about the Internet in their book *The New Digital Age*: "It is a source for tremendous good and potentially dreadful evil, and we're only just beginning to witness its impact on the world stage."[6]

CHAPTER ONE

The Threat from Sexual Predators

Online sexual predators target girls, boys, men, and women of all ages in a variety of ways and for a variety of reasons. Their motives range from having pathological sexual desires to seeking money, power, and revenge. Both the far reach of the Internet and the popularity of mobile digital devices have made it easy for pedophiles and other sexual predators to find and lure their victims and to share pornography and personal information with other predators. Thus, the number of these criminals continues to grow. The FBI estimates that at least 750,000 sexual predators are online at any given moment.

Law enforcement experts are most concerned about sexual predators who target children and teenagers. Technically, predators who target preadolescent kids are defined as pedophiles, while those who target teenagers and adults are called sexual predators. According to the National Center for Missing & Exploited Children, 76 percent of sexual predators' victims are abused before they reach puberty, 24 percent have reached puberty, and 10 percent are infants and toddlers. In 2013 the center received ten thousand to thirteen thousand tips on possible instances of online sexual abuse. The center's records indicate that these numbers increase each year.

The National Center for Missing and Exploited Children receives thousands of tips about possible online sexual abuse. The map located behind the agency's chief operating officer, Michelle DeLaune, shows locations where reported incidents occurred.

Who Are Sexual Predators?

Pedophiles and other sexual predators flourish online because hiding behind a screen name gives them an extra layer of protection. Such anonymity lets them pretend to be whomever they think will most attract specific individuals. For example, if a predator's target is a thirteen-year-old girl, the person might pretend to be a slightly older teenage boy. If the target is an older man, the predator might pretend to be a woman. People of all ages and all walks of life have taken advantage of this anonymity. As FBI special agent Dan Evans noted in a 2013 NBC 7 San Diego interview, "Online predators now are everybody. They're not just the creepy-looking guy that everyone associates [the term] with. A 13-year-old girl can be your online predator."[7]

Cybersecurity experts say it is especially difficult for law enforcement and potential victims to identify predators because they are experienced con artists who switch identities or screen names as needed. For example, Lucas Michael Chansler used about 150 different screen names, including "Cuddley" and "Good Looking Guy," from 2007 to 2010. Chansler was in his twenties when he victimized at least 350 girls aged thirteen to eighteen who lived in the United States, England, and Canada. He convincingly pretended to be a fifteen-year-old boy, and his victims had no reason to suspect otherwise. He later told the FBI that he targeted teenaged girls because he thought adult women were too smart to fall for his con.

No matter who they pretend to be online, sexual predators come in all shapes and sizes and hail from many walks of life. They can be students, teachers, doctors, police officers, clergy members, or in any other line of work; they may be teenagers, adults, or elderly. Many have no criminal record because they excel in eluding police. They often appear to be kind and caring. Many are even prominent citizens. The thing they all have in common is that they are skilled at deceiving others and use well-rehearsed tactics to lure and abuse their victims. According to the FBI, they are all "master manipulators."[8]

> "Online predators now are everybody. They're not just the creepy-looking guy that everyone associates [the term] with. A 13-year-old girl can be your online predator."[7]
>
> —FBI special agent Dan Evans.

Heightened Vulnerability

Although sexual predators and pedophiles have always victimized youth, law enforcement and child welfare experts warn that the Internet has made children and teens more vulnerable than ever to predators, who seek pornographic photos, videos, and sexual encounters. This is mostly because smartphones, webcams, gaming devices, and social media sites give predators unprecedented access to young people and allow them to interact with their victims every day. According to the FBI, "Pedophiles go where children are. Before the Internet, that meant places such as amusement parks and zoos. Today, the virtual world makes it alarmingly simple for pedophiles—often pretending to be teens themselves—to make contact with young people."[9]

Before smartphones and other small digital devices became popular, most families had one shared computer. Hence, it was relatively easy for parents to install filtering software and monitor their children's computer use. Modern mobile digital devices, however, make it easy for kids to conceal their online activities from their parents. In fact, many parents have no idea that their children have shared personal information and posted revealing photos of themselves. A 2013 study from computer security software company McAfee, for example, found that only 8 percent of parents of young people ages thirteen to twenty-three are aware that their children have posted intimate photos on social media sites. Furthermore, 69 percent of children and teens say they hide their online activities from their parents. For instance, the McAfee study found that 48 percent of teens regularly clear their browser history, 32 percent delete or hide instant messages, and 9 percent disable parental controls.

Psychologists say that most children and teens lack the real-world experience to be aware of just how many determined and demented predators are hanging out online, waiting for others to post personal details and photos. Few teens realize that when they post nude photos of themselves on Snapchat, for example, thousands of predators could potentially view them. "Users think their snaps will disappear and they are wrong," explains Ann Brenoff, a columnist for the *Huffington Post*. "It's actually pretty easy to recover a snap, take a screenshot of it and share it with others—and by others we mean porn sites."[10] Thus, photos that teens think they are sharing only with friends end up in the digital files of sexual predators all over the world.

> "Pedophiles go where children are. Before the Internet, that meant places such as amusement parks and zoos. Today, the virtual world makes it alarmingly simple for pedophiles— often pretending to be teens themselves—to make contact with young people."[9]
>
> —The FBI.

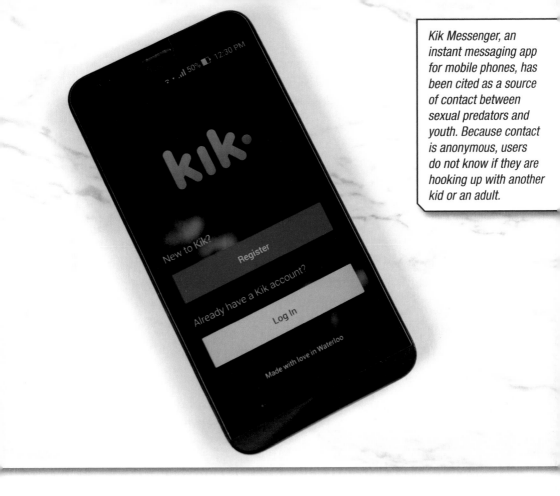

Kik Messenger, an instant messaging app for mobile phones, has been cited as a source of contact between sexual predators and youth. Because contact is anonymous, users do not know if they are hooking up with another kid or an adult.

Sexual predators also connect with kids by using social media apps—particularly Kik Messenger, an instant messaging app for mobile phones. Many tweens and teens use Kik to hook up with others they assume are peers. But Kik and similar apps allow sexual predators to troll for victims while remaining anonymous. Predators also take advantage of Kik's role-playing feature, which helps the predator create a profile that is most likely to attract the type of child he or she desires. Indeed, in 2015 a convicted pedophile sent a journalist a letter that revealed how he and other pedophiles use Kik. The letter contained a plea to parents that stated, "Please, delete this app off your kids' phone."[11]

Common Sexual Predators' Schemes

Online sexual predators use other technologies and methods to target and lure their victims, too. The most common and predictable method involves hanging out on gaming websites, social media sites, and chat rooms that children and teenagers use, then targeting and grooming a victim.

Many predators target kids who seem unsure of themselves, crave attention, or are caught up in traumatic family situations. Some target kids who live nearby, to make it easier to arrange in-person encounters. In one case a teenaged Massachusetts girl wrote in a chat room that she was "small and lost"[12] and wanted to run away from home. A New York couple established an online relationship with her, then kidnapped and sexually abused her. "Unfortunately, predators can smell a child who is vulnerable, it's like chum to a shark,"[13] states Parry Aftab, director of the Internet safety organization Cyberangels.

> "Predators can smell a child who is vulnerable, it's like chum to a shark."[13]
>
> —Parry Aftab, director of the Internet safety organization Cyberangels.

After making contact, the predator begins the grooming process, which is the systematic method by which a predator establishes a relationship and lowers the victim's inhibitions about sexual encounters. Many predators pose as teenagers and follow a carefully thought-out plan to gain the victim's trust. They learn to speak and write the way kids do online, using popular abbreviations and code words, such as KPC (keep parents clueless), code 9 (parents are around), and GNOC (get naked on cam). They keep up with contemporary musicians, actors, and games so they appear to be peers or slightly older friends. For instance, pedophile Robert Hunter of Great Britain pretended to be Justin Bieber to convince young girls all over the world to perform sex acts in front of a webcam.

Most predators also flatter their victims excessively and seem sympathetic to problems the victim may be having with family, friends, or in school. In 2015, for example, a fifteen-year-old Ohio girl's troubles led her to use Kik Messenger to meet a man whom she thought was in his twenties. She was unhappy because her stepfather had recently died and her mother had already moved in with a new boyfriend. Her new online "friend" seemed compas-

An Antipredator App

Sexual predators often use social media apps to find and abuse their victims, but law enforcement agents fight back with apps of their own. One of the most effective predator-tracking apps is RADAR, developed in 2008 by Robert Lotter, CEO of the mobile device security company eAgency. RADAR has a 100 percent conviction rate in the thousands of cases in which it has been used. eAgency provides it free to law enforcement departments.

Lotter created RADAR after a detective at the Orange County, California, sheriff's department, where Lotter volunteered, told him about the problem of online sexual abuse. "When I realized how easy it was to exploit children, I made it my personal mission in life to stop this kind of evil from happening," Lotter told *Newsweek*.

At that time, no reliable methods of gathering evidence from cell phones existed. Lotter and his team modified an existing mobile phone app to create RADAR, which tracks and logs phone calls, texts, and online conversations. Once an arrest is made, RADAR delivers a chronological accounting of all the evidence gathered during an investigation. This is important in proving cases in court, since without impeccable documentation, defense attorneys can accuse police of tampering with evidence.

In one 2014 Illinois case, police placed RADAR on a twelve-year-old girl's phone after she reported being victimized by an online sexual predator. After pedophile Bryan Woldman, a thirty-six-year-old personal trainer, arranged to meet the girl in person at a local movie theater, police—who were monitoring the girl's phone—arrested him at the theater.

Quoted in Tracey Harrington McCoy, "The Sexual Predator App with a 100 Percent Conviction Rate," *Newsweek*, August 18, 2014. www.newsweek.com.

sionate and offered to help her, so she willingly got into his car when he arrived at her house. In reality, he was a forty-one-year-old predator named Christopher Schroeder, who drove her to his home in Missouri and raped her.

The grooming process can proceed quickly or slowly, depending on how long it takes the predator to gain the victim's trust. Once trust has been established, the predator gradually introduces sexual topics and pornography either to coax, force, or blackmail the victim into having an in-person sexual encounter or providing explicit photos and videos. Some reveal their true age to the victim before an in-person meeting and may use their status as an adult to force the victim to comply with their demands. Others perpetuate the ruse of being a peer until an in-person meeting takes place.

Many predators practice sextortion, in which they force their victims to send them sexually explicit photos and videos to avoid certain consequences. For example, in 2012 a thirty-five-year-old Dutch predator named Aydin Coban threatened to harm fifteen-year-old Amanda Todd and her family unless she complied with his requests to send him nude videos of herself. Coban then post-

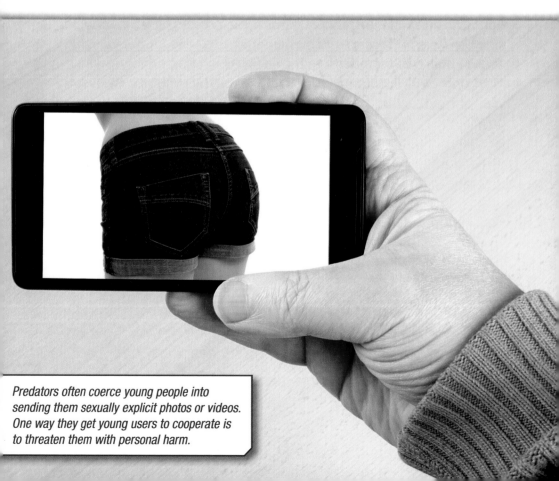

Predators often coerce young people into sending them sexually explicit photos or videos. One way they get young users to cooperate is to threaten them with personal harm.

ed the videos online. When Todd moved to a new place, Coban tracked her online and intensified his demands until, as the result of a variety of factors, Todd eventually killed herself.

Chansler, on the other hand, conned his victims into posing naked during video chats. During the chats, he secretly took screenshots, which he used to blackmail his victims into posing in increasingly pornographic ways. If they refused, he vowed to send the screenshots to the girls' friends and parents. One of Chansler's victims, Ashley Reynolds, described the relentlessness with which she was pursued. "He was not going to stop and he was set on sharing my picture with whoever he could to ruin my reputation,"[14] she stated.

Money and Pornography

Other predators extort money from their victims. In one case, eighteen-year-old Yanick Paré of Canada thought he was in an online relationship with a woman named Sandra Roy. When she asked him to join her in some intimate webcam activities, he did so. But "Sandra" was a fake social media profile created by two predators from Burkina Faso in Africa. They recorded the webcam video and soon informed Paré that they would share it with his family and friends unless he sent them thousands of dollars. They threatened to make the video look like he was masturbating in front of a nine-year-old girl. He sent the money, but they kept demanding more. Paré eventually killed himself.

Other predators engage in moneymaking schemes that involve selling online pornography. Authorities are especially concerned about the explosion of online pedophile networks that share and sell child pornography. Some of these networks conduct their business through private Facebook groups, while others have websites devoted to the sale of child pornography.

An increasing number of these online businesses involve pedophiles paying to view videos of other pedophiles raping young children. This has become increasingly prevalent since Internet access became available worldwide and since more and more computers have webcams. A 2014 Bloomberg Technology article

Human Trafficking

Human trafficking involves kidnapping, selling, and forcing men, women, and children to become sex slaves. While human trafficking has occurred throughout history, modern technology has exponentially increased the ability of human traffickers to prey on victims.

In one case that affected hundreds of teenaged girls in northern Virginia, Justin Strom, leader of the Underground Gangster Crips sex-trafficking ring, was sentenced to forty years in prison in 2012 after several victims turned him in. Strom and his gang trolled social media sites, looking for potential victims. They then used fake identities and contacted girls they determined were likely prospects, based on the girls' postings that indicated friction with parents, a desire for expensive clothes, and other qualities. The gang flattered the girls and eventually offered them a chance to make money. Many girls willingly met Strom in person. Once a girl was in his car, he and other gang members drugged her and took her to a home, where they raped her and informed her that she would be used as a prostitute. Girls who resisted were hit, knifed, raped, threatened, and drugged into submission. One girl who testified at Strom's trial said he forced her to have sex with five, ten, or more men each day. These activities went on for six years before several victims helped police build a case against these predators, which led to their arrest.

explains that "as Internet access spreads in countries like the Philippines, Thailand and Sri Lanka, children as young as infants are molested and raped on demand by family members and criminal groups for customers on the other side of the lens."[15] Children's rights advocate Hans Guyt told Bloomberg Technology that these abuses are "fueled by poverty at home and predators around the world with $100 to spare to watch a child get raped."[16]

Other predators use pornography to make money in different ways. For example, in 2012 Kevin Bollaert of San Diego, California, set up what is known as a revenge-porn site called

UGotPosted.com. It contained thousands of pornographic photos of women, teens, and young girls that he stole from other websites or that revenge-seeking ex-lovers posted on his site. Victims were publicly shamed and exposed, because anyone who posted photos to the site was required to include the subject's name, age, and area of residence, plus links to the subject's Facebook profile.

Then Bollaert set up a second website called ChangeMy Reputation.com, on which he offered to remove the photos from the porn site for $250 to $350. He found that the more public harassment the female victims endured from the porn site postings, the more each was willing to pay to remove the photos. Bollaert earned about $30,000 from ChangeMyReputation.com before police finally shut down the sites and arrested him in 2013. In April 2015 he was sentenced to eighteen years in jail and ordered to pay $15,000 in restitution to each victim, in addition to a $10,000 fine.

Effects on Victims

The effects on Bollaert's victims, however, could never be undone by monetary restitution alone. Like other victims of online sexual predators, many lost their jobs and faced traumatic taunting from Internet trolls and in-person shamers. Many received so many threats in their hometowns that they had to move. Some received hundreds of messages from people who wanted to hook up with them. One victim felt so humiliated that she quit college and spent time in a mental hospital. Another tried to kill herself. As one victim whose family threw her out of their home told the court during Bollaert's case, "It ruined my life and I'm still going through it. I lost my family. They think that I brought shame on them. My reputation is ruined."[17]

> "It ruined my life and I'm still going through it. I lost my family. They think that I brought shame on them. My reputation is ruined."[17]
>
> —Female victim of revenge-porn website designer Kevin Bollaert.

No matter what form the sexual abuse takes, the emotional and physical effects on victims are serious and even life-threatening.

Feelings of terror, anxiety, and depression are common. Ashley Reynolds, who was fourteen when she became one of Chansler's victims, told CBS News she was terrified by Chansler's threats and felt like "a slave."[18]

These feelings are often exacerbated by victims' efforts to hide what is going on from their families and others around them. Research by experts such as David Finkelhor of the Crimes Against Children Research Center indicates that few children and teens who find themselves trapped by a sexual predator tell their parents because of threats by the predator, shame or guilt, or fears that they will lose their computer or smartphone privileges. But hiding what they are enduring usually involves lying and withdrawing from family and friends.

Many victims also find that their peers react to their abuse by further abusing, isolating, rejecting, or harassing them. For instance, before Amanda Todd killed herself, her classmates bullied her online and in person, telling her that she had asked for the abuse. This led her to abuse alcohol and drugs and to cut herself. According to the US Department of Justice's National Sex Offender Public Website, these are common coping behaviors for victims of sexual predators. When Todd attempted suicide by drinking bleach, her pain intensified when numerous classmates posted online comments encouraging her to try again. This was one of many incidents that compounded Todd's devastation from her online sexual abuse and led her to eventually kill herself. For other victims, the effects of online sexual abuse can last a lifetime.

CHAPTER TWO

Tricks and Technologies Used by Online Predators

As more people use the Internet for banking, record keeping, shopping, and other finance-related activities, more and more become vulnerable to hackers and identity thieves. In 2014 about 17.6 million Americans were victims of identity theft, which the Bureau of Justice Statistics defines as the "unauthorized use or attempted use of an existing account, unauthorized use or attempted use of personal information to open a new account, [or] misuse of personal information for a fraudulent purpose."[19]

Of these victims, 64 percent reported direct financial losses, with the amount averaging $1,343 per person. Many also reported indirect losses, such as legal fees incurred for representation, bank fees for bounced checks, and time taken off work to resolve theft-related problems. Debts incurred by cyberthieves also caused victims to be unable to get new credit cards or loans; other victims had their utilities shut off, and still others were harassed by bill collectors.

Some hackers who steal identities, money, or other sensitive or valuable information do so out of greed or revenge, while others do so in pursuit of a religious, political, or social agenda. Whatever their motives, the payoffs can be huge; hackers who breach a personal computer can gain access to the owner's Social Security number, bank account numbers, credit card accounts, passwords, and other personal information. Hacking into a large business or government computer network often yields similar information regarding thousands or even millions of people, along with secret business or government data. No matter the size or scale of a breach, all types of identity and financial theft are of major concern. As the FBI puts it, "A stolen identity is a powerful cloak of anonymity for criminals and terrorists . . . and a danger to national security and private citizens alike."[20]

Phishing, Smishing, Vishing, and Twishing

Hackers often operate by getting around a computer's or network's firewalls, antimalware software, and other defense mechanisms. *Malware* refers to any type of malicious code, such as viruses, worms, bots, and spyware, that a predator places on a computer without the owner's permission. Malware can delete computer files, ruin an entire hard drive, encrypt (scramble) data, or allow a predator to follow a computer user's keystrokes and online activities.

> "A stolen identity is a powerful cloak of anonymity for criminals and terrorists . . . and a danger to national security and private citizens alike."[20]
>
> —The FBI.

Most hackers engage in phishing, which is a general term for trying to trick a victim into revealing confidential personal information. Variations on phishing include smishing (a phishing attack delivered via texting); vishing (which features phone calls made over the Internet); and twishing (which sends malware through Twitter). Whether phishing, smishing, vishing, or twishing, a predator's goal is to con victims via spam e-mails, phone calls, or phony websites.

A common smishing ploy involves a hacker sending a text that reads something like, "Thank you for signing up. You will be charged $5 per day unless you click on this link to cancel."[21] Clicking on the link provided then downloads malware to the victim's device. Vishing predators, meanwhile, use caller-ID spoofing to make it appear that the call is from a legitimate source to increase

the chances the victim will answer and be persuaded to reveal credit card or other sensitive information. In one vishing scheme, telemarketers made millions of robocalls (automatically dialed calls that deliver a prerecorded message) on behalf of the Transcontinental Warranty Company of Florida, which sold bogus extended car warranties. The message instructed victims to call a toll-free number to buy an extended warranty—at a cost of $2,000 to $3,000—to replace the existing warranty that was about to expire. The victim was then instructed to type in a credit card number.

In one common phishing scam, predators send e-mails that look like they come from a trusted source, such as a bank. Opening the e-mail or clicking on an enclosed link may take the victim to a phony website that looks identical to that of the victim's bank. When the victim signs in with his or her user name and password, the predator steals the information and accesses the victim's real account via the bank's real website. In a different scam perpetrated by six Estonian cyberthieves, phishing e-mails were sent to millions of computers belonging to iTunes customers. The e-mails contained a virus that diverted victims to a fake website when they tried to log on to the real iTunes site. The victim would then pay for merchandise that was never delivered, and the thieves stole the customers' credit card numbers. This not only hurt the victims, but also resulted in lost business for iTunes.

In yet other scams, predators do what is called session phishing, in which they infect a browser such as Firefox with malware. This causes a pop-up window to appear soon after a victim accesses a legitimate website that requires the user to sign in. The pop-up states something like, "Your session has expired. Please re-type your user ID and password."[22] When the user does so, the predator steals the information. It can be difficult for victims to recognize this as a scam, since many websites, including banking and credit card sites, use pop-ups to let customers know that their online session is expiring.

Predators also use software that guesses passwords to hack into victims' e-mail accounts. The predator then impersonates the victim and sends phishing e-mails with infected links to everyone on the victim's contact list. Many contacts open such e-mails because they think a trusted friend sent them. In other cases hackers use the information they find in a private e-mail account to blackmail or otherwise extort the owner of the account. This is what Ryan Collins of Lancaster, Pennsylvania, did when he obtained user names and passwords for Apple and Google account holders—mostly female celebrities, including actress Jennifer Lawrence and model Kate Upton—between November 2012 and September 2014. He hacked into the women's iCloud or Gmail accounts and stole nude photos and videos, which he posted online.

Scareware is another variation on phishing. In this scam pop-ups warn victims that their computer is infected and that they must click on a link to diagnose the problem. Then the victim is told to download a tool to scrub out the virus. The download looks like it comes from a legitimate source, such as the Microsoft Internet Safety and Security Center, so many people fall for this ploy and end up downloading malware. The thieves also steal

Data Packets: The Key to Internet Communications and Hacking

The technologies that underlie the Internet originated in 1969 when the US government launched the Advanced Research Projects Agency Network (ARPANET) program to develop a secure worldwide communications network for the military. One concept that scientists incorporated into ARPANET was the Galactic Network idea, which suggested that a network could be used to electronically link computers worldwide so they could share information.

In 1965 Lawrence Roberts of the Massachusetts Institute of Technology tried to launch a Galactic Network by using a telephone line to connect a computer in Massachusetts with one in California. However, Roberts realized that telephone circuit switches were too slow to allow high-speed computer networking. He consulted with scientists who were developing packet switches, which group digital data into small units (packets). Roberts soon discovered that packet switches allowed much faster data transmission. He and his associates therefore incorporated packet switches into the ARPANET.

The Internet that grew out of ARPANET also uses packets of data, and many malicious hacking techniques involve manipulating packets. Hackers often use software that hijacks packets as they travel between website servers and users or between e-mail senders and receivers. Some hackers create false packets that trick recipients into accepting a connection to the hacker's computer. Others tamper with packet-routing instruction codes to route messages to their own computers. Other times, hackers use "sniffing" software to detect vulnerabilities in servers' coded commands and insert their own commands to gain control.

the credit card number the victim uses to pay for the "computer cleaning." A variation on scareware is called clickjacking, in which victims attempt to banish a pop-up by clicking on the red X in the corner and end up downloading malware.

Hacking Vulnerable Websites

Rather than conning victims by phishing, some hackers find and exploit computer security vulnerabilities. These refer to the small coding errors, or bugs, that every computer program contains. Some hackers use special software that looks for these errors, which may involve weaknesses in the code that regulates how data is sent from a server to a browser or how data is encrypted.

Once these hackers find such weak spots, they write computer code that allows them to break into the site's databases and steal information like user names and passwords. Usually, the most vulnerable websites are government, social media, and e-mail server sites, which are deliberately engineered to be accessible to the public. In 2014, for example, a Russian crime ring used these techniques to steal 1.2 billion people's names and passwords from more than 400,000 social media and e-mail servers' sites.

A different type of hack exploits vulnerabilities in code that governs how computers connect and how data is encrypted. In April 2014 nineteen-year-old Stephen Solis-Reyes of Ontario, Canada, was one of many hackers to use this technique to exploit the so-called Heartbleed bug to steal information from numerous websites, including the Canada Revenue Agency site. The bug was in the OpenSSL software program that millions of websites use to encrypt data that is sent between a server and a browser. OpenSSL creates a secure connection between the server and browser by generating a digital signal called a heartbeat, which lets the computer on each end know that the other is still there. The heartbeat contains two elements: a data packet called the payload and information about the payload's size. The Heartbleed bug allowed hackers to insert code that falsified the payload size. This prompted the server to add, or "bleed," data from its memory into the heartbeat to send back the correct amount of

> "At the end of the day, these open government networks are vulnerable to these kinds of things. They're very accessible and they let in a lot of traffic because they have to manage large volumes."[23]
>
> —Ray Boisvert, security expert.

payload data. This data could contain information like user names, passwords, and digital keys that decrypted the data.

Computer detectives have traced many such schemes to hackers employed by the Chinese or North Korean governments. However, aside from fixing security flaws, government officials say there is little they can do to prevent these attacks. "At the end of the day, these open government networks are vulnerable to these kinds of things," explains Ray Boisvert, a security expert. "They're very accessible and they let in a lot of traffic because they have to manage large volumes."[23]

Impersonators and Other Actor-Predators

Some hackers don't steal information; instead they pretend to be a trusted authority or entity and get people to volunteer their information, money, or both. For example, ploys exist in which hackers impersonate the FBI, the Internal Revenue Service (IRS), or another government agency and scare victims into sending money

The Heartbleed bug enabled hackers to steal information from many websites. Among those targeted was the Canadian government's Revenue Agency. The heartbleed.com website (pictured) provides information on the bug and on how a patch, or fix, can correct it.

to supposedly avoid being fined or arrested. Or a predator will claim via e-mail, text message, or phone call that he or she is with the victim's bank and needs to verify account information to avoid closing the account. Although banks and government offices inform customers that they will never call or e-mail to verify account numbers or passwords, thousands of people fall for these schemes.

Some impersonators try to get victims to wire money directly to the predator's bank account. Once this happens, the predator disappears and the victim cannot recover the money. In one common scenario, the predator e-mails or calls to inform a victim that he or she has won a huge lottery prize but must wire money to cover taxes and fees associated with the "prize" before being paid. In a similar scam, an e-mail might state that a generous Nigerian prince has chosen to share a fortune with the victim if he or she first wires money to cover taxes.

In yet another impersonation scam, a predator who has stolen someone's Social Security number might file a fake online income tax return and claim he or she is owed a refund. The government then sends the refund electronically to the thief's bank account, and it is only when the real owner of the Social Security number files for a refund that he or she finds out what has happened. This happened in April 2015, when Eric and Lauren Oxford of Massachusetts discovered that a cyberthief had stolen Eric's Social Security number and filed a fraudulent tax return claiming money the Oxfords were owed. The IRS told the Oxfords it could take six or more months to obtain their refund, given the huge backlog of fraud cases being processed. Indeed, in 2015 alone the IRS confirmed that 16,523 fraudulent tax returns involved identity theft.

Many predators who impersonate others also use call-spoofing software or spoofing cards that make phone calls or text messages appear to come from a number other than that of the predator. For example, a predator might hack into someone's contact list and spoof, or mimic, the name and number of a relative or friend so the victim will answer the call. Some spoof the number of a local police department and tell the victim that he or she will be imprisoned unless payments for, say, unpaid traffic tickets are wired immediately.

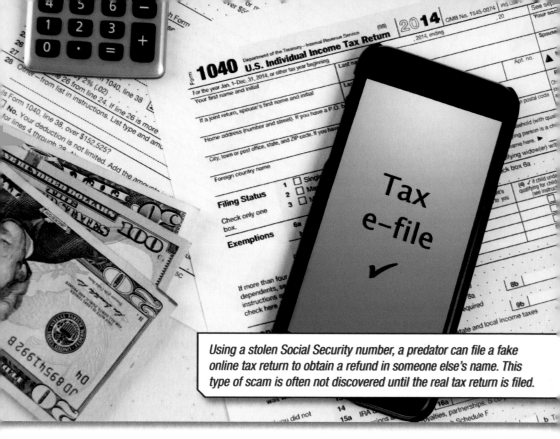

Using a stolen Social Security number, a predator can file a fake online tax return to obtain a refund in someone else's name. This type of scam is often not discovered until the real tax return is filed.

Spoof cards are illegal in the United States, but many predators buy them from overseas vendors. Police say it is difficult to catch call spoofers since they often buy the cards using a fake name and make calls from disposable cell phones.

Preying on Human Compassion

Some online predators prey on the goodwill of decent people by pretending, say, to be a victim of tragic circumstances. They then exploit a victim's emotional response to extort money. In one such case a woman who claimed her name was Mary joined an online women's support group in California. She told group members that her husband beat her and had forced her out of their home. She claimed she had no money and was living on the streets. Compassionate group members responded by sending her thousands of dollars.

After one group member, Melissa Nester, met Mary in person and realized she was a con artist, Mary told Nester she would ruin

Hackers and Crackers

Even though the term *hacker* usually has a negative connotation, computer experts emphasize that most hackers are white hat, or constructive, hackers who use their knowledge and skills to build computer security systems. In fact, the word *hacker* originated in the 1960s to describe programmers who hacked out computer code and launched new types of computer programs and applications. Early hacks were actually shortcuts designed to simplify or improve computer programs.

When networks that linked small numbers of computers became operational, hackers began devising ways to breach these networks, mostly out of curiosity to determine how they worked. During the 1980s hacker groups and clubs became popular. Most consisted of teenagers and young adults who competitively honed their skills. Some began hacking into secure government and military databases via the new Internet. For example, in 1988 the infamous teenage hacker Kevin Poulsen broke into secret government files and also stole sensitive information from phone companies. He cleverly eluded capture by the FBI for several years. Also in 1988, Cornell University graduate student and hacker Robert Morris developed and launched one of the first computer worms, which earned him a felony conviction under the 1986 Computer Fraud and Abuse Act.

As Internet use grew throughout the 1990s, black-hat, or malicious, hackers launched increasingly sophisticated cyberattacks to steal data and information and to commit other crimes. Many security experts prefer to call these malicious hackers *crackers*, since they crack open computer systems that aim to keep them out.

her life unless she kept her mouth shut and kept giving her money. Nester refused, and Mary carried out her threat. She set up fake e-mail and social media accounts and even websites and used them to portray Nester as a prostitute and drug dealer. Nester lost many friends and even her job. When she applied for a new one, prospective employers refused to hire her after searching for her name online.

Keylogging

Another predatory method hackers use is keylogging. This involves installing malware or hardware on a computer that then allows a thief to monitor the machine's activity. Keylogging has legitimate uses, such as when parents wish to track their children's online activities. But predators also use this technique to steal valuable information. A predator may secretly attach a keylogging USB cable to a computer or install keylogging malware from a distance by conning the victim into downloading an infected e-mail attachment. As McAfee security expert Robert Siciliano puts it, "Whether it is called a keylogger, spyware or monitoring software, it can be the equivalent of digital surveillance, revealing every click and touch, every download and conversation."[24] Most victims are unaware they have been targeted. Those who suspect something may change their passwords, but they may not realize the keylogger can see these changes being made.

"Whether it is called a keylogger, spyware or monitoring software, it can be the equivalent of digital surveillance, revealing every click and touch, every download and conversation."[24]

—Robert Siciliano, McAfee security expert.

Although many predatory keyloggers are strangers, some are family members, friends, or others who have physical access to the victim's computer. In one case a young woman named Marita stole more than $100,000 from her parents' retirement accounts and racked up tens of thousands of dollars in credit card charges after her boyfriend installed keylogging hardware on the parents' computer. When her parents confronted her, Marita waved them off and said, "That money was coming to me when you die."[25]

Ransomware

Another tool cyberthieves use is ransomware. This software hacks into electronic databases and encrypts the data, then demands a ransom to decrypt and return the files. Encryption is usually used to protect sensitive data from being unscrambled and accessed by unauthorized people, but cyberthieves have corrupted this traditional security measure and used it for blackmail.

Like other malware, ransomware usually gets into computers through infected e-mails or links. Police departments, hospitals, and many other institutions and businesses have been targeted. In one case an employee at a town government office in Mahone Bay, Canada, clicked on a malicious e-mail and accidentally infected the company's computer network with ransomware called CryptoWall. The malware arrived in an e-mail marked "Resumé," and the employee opened it because the agency was in fact looking to hire new employees. CryptoWall did its damage over several days, and a technician was called in when certain files could not be accessed. The technician discovered a ransom note demanding three bitcoins—about $900. Bitcoins are a difficult-to-trace online currency often used by cybercriminals.

Some victims pay the ransom to get back important files. The Mahone Bay victims chose not to pay because the affected files were not critical. Other victims escape the need to pay up because they have proactively backed up data on external hard drives or data sticks. The FBI urges all computer users to take this precaution, since receiving ransoms encourages cyberthieves to victimize more people.

Many security experts say crime that features ransomware is the fastest-growing cybercrime. Indeed, in 2015 the FBI received reports of about twenty-five hundred ransomware attacks that cost American victims a collective $24 million. By 2016 ransomware attacks had grown exponentially; victims had already paid out $209 million by the end of March. Many attacks go unreported, so the real cost is probably higher.

As fast as authorities find ways to block ransomware, malware, keylogging software, phishing e-mails, and other scams, new, harder-to-block software emerges. This is why computer security and law enforcement experts face ongoing and seemingly unending challenges in the battle to gain the upper hand against online predators.

CHAPTER THREE

Data Breaches and Identity Theft

Online hackers and identity thieves employ many methods to commit a range of crimes. Very often such crimes are financial in nature—stealing money from bank accounts, shopping with stolen credit or debit card numbers, or even taking out home mortgages in a victim's name. Other crimes involve stealing personal and medical information from electronic medical files and using this information to impersonate a patient or blackmail a health care provider. But no matter what the criminal's motives or methods, the effects on victims can be devastating.

Financial Cyberthieves

Thieves have always sought to separate people from their money. But technology has made thieves' jobs easier by giving them access to far more victims than in pre-Internet times, when a criminal usually had to actually go to the place they were robbing. The Internet has also allowed thieves to have an international reach, as they can now easily conduct long-distance robberies from anywhere in the world. Indeed, most cyberthieves operate from India, eastern Europe, Turkey, China, Pakistan, and several other areas, though many are certainly active in the United States as well. According to a cybersecurity report by Akamai Technologies, during a three-month period in 2013, 33 percent of cyberattacks originated from China. The second-largest source of attacks (12 percent), was the United States, followed by Russia, Taiwan, and Turkey (5 percent from each).

In one particularly devastating string of thefts, a worldwide ring of thieves led by Turkish cyberpredator Ercan Findikoglu hacked into debit card payment processors' computer networks. They raised the balances and withdrawal limits on thousands of prepaid Visa, MasterCard, JPMorgan Chase, and other debit cards. They then made physical copies of these cards and, armed with card owners' personal identification numbers, went to ATMs and withdrew millions of dollars in cash from 2010 to 2013. In a February 2013 attack on New York City, ring members stole more than $2.4 million from three thousand ATMs in a single day. Findikoglu, whose aliases included Segate, Predator, and Orean, eventually pled guilty to numerous counts of fraud in March 2016 after being extradited to the United States from Germany.

Perpetrators Can Be Business Associates or Best Friends

It is not just crime rings that steal data, money, and information—such things are also frequently stolen by people loosely involved with an organization or company, such as contractors or business associates. One increasingly common source of business associate–related hacks are employees of overseas customer-service call centers that numerous American companies have set up in India and Pakistan. When customers give their account numbers to customer-service associates, these employees have easy access to information, which some have used to steal money and/or identities. In one 2005 incident, for example, employees of a Citibank customer service center in Pune, India, stole $350,000 from four customers in New York.

Other times, hackers may pretend to be business associates in order to gain access to a system, as happened in the 2013 Target data theft in which hackers stole the credit card information of more than 40 million Target customers. The Target hackers pretended to work for a refrigerator vendor with which Target does business. The loss was substantial both for the victims and

Thieves have found ways to get money out of ATM accounts. Sometimes they do this with stolen personal identification numbers but this type of theft can be accomplished even without those numbers.

for Target, as many of the affected customers terminated their accounts and shopped elsewhere. This cost the company billions of dollars in revenue and damaged its reputation.

Although many financial cybercrimes are committed under the guise of business, sometimes victims are betrayed by those closest to them. Indeed, family members, friends, or ex-spouses or lovers have been responsible for numerous instances of financial cybercrime. For example, after Alexis Moore, coauthor of the book *Cyber Self-Defense*, left her abusive boyfriend, he took advantage of their former closeness to steal all the money from her bank accounts, run up huge bills on her credit cards, and destroy her credit rating to get back at her for leaving. He also tapped her phone and cyberstalked her every move to enhance her fear of him. "There was one person with enough information on me and knowledge of how to work the system to do this: my ex," writes Moore. "I had a worst-case scenario cyberstalker—a man who knew all my passwords, addresses, birth date, mother's maiden name—all the personal stuff that makes up our technological identity. He was determined to use all of his knowledge against me."[26] It took Moore four years to undo the financial damage and to recover physically and emotionally from the ordeal.

Homeless Homeowners

Some cyberthieves steal more than money or personal information. An increasingly prevalent practice involves stealing homes from homeowners. The scam works like this: Thieves browse publically accessible online home ownership records, steal enough personal information from a homeowner to impersonate or otherwise steal his or her identity, and forge the homeowner's signature on legal forms that transfer home ownership. Sometimes the thief then sells the property and pockets the profits, leaving the real homeowner homeless or stuck paying a mortgage.

> "To steal a house, a thief only needs some public information found easily online, ten minutes Photoshopping a fake deed, and a trip to one of our offices to record their false ownership."[27]
>
> —Karen Yarbrough, Cook County, Illinois, property deed recorder.

Many local and county governments have established fraud units to specifically deal with these offenses. Karen Yarbrough, the Cook County, Illinois, property deed recorder, has warned local residents that it is much easier to steal a house than a car because car thieves must take physical possession of the vehicle. "To steal a car, you have to make sure nobody is around, pry open a door or break a window, and if there is no alarm, find a way to get it started, which isn't easy with anti-theft technology today," says Yarbrough. "To steal a house, a thief only needs some public information found easily online, ten minutes Photoshopping a fake deed, and a trip to one of our offices to record their false ownership."[27]

Sometimes, predators target vacant homes to prevent occupants from getting suspicious. Other times, they target elderly people who have paid off their mortgages and own the property free and clear. This makes it easier for the thief, who does not have to worry about a mortgage lender questioning the sale of the home.

The Vulnerable Cloud

One factor that contributes to many data breaches is the increasing amount of data stored in the cloud. Cloud servers allow computer users to free up operating and hard drive space by storing data with companies like Google Drive and Dropbox, which specialize in safe-keeping it. According to the Center for Democracy & Technology, "Cloud computing can offer increased computing speed, capacity flexibility, and security at significantly lower cost."

But many public-access cloud servers allow all Internet users or all computer network participants to access their websites—which makes the data vulnerable to identity thieves. Private cloud servers, on the other hand, are more secure, but they can be costly. But even private servers are not immune to hacking. A 2015 report by the Alert Logic security company stated that cloud servers experienced a 45 percent increase in hacker attacks in 2014. "Hackers, like everyone else, have a limited amount of time to complete their job," the report explained. "They want to invest their time and resources into attacks that will bear the most fruit: businesses using cloud environments are largely considered that fruit-bearing jackpot."

Center for Democracy & Technology, "FAQ: HIPAA and Cloud Computing," August 7, 2013. www.cdt.org.

Quoted in Danny Palmer, "Hackers See Cloud as 'a Fruit-Bearing Jackpot' for Cyber Attacks," *Computing*, October 6, 2015. www.computing.co.uk.

In one such case an elderly woman called the Cook County Property Fraud Unit to report that a man was changing the locks on her door after showing her a document that claimed he owned her house. The fraud unit investigated and called police, who arrested the thief a week later after discovering that he had filed numerous false changes of ownership. A judge declared the recorded document to be fraudulent, and the true owner got her home back. But other victims have not been able to prove fraud and have lost their homes.

Medical Data Hacking

Online predators do not go after only bank accounts and homes, however. In fact, another growing target of online theft is medical data, which is used to steal individuals' identities and even blackmail individuals into giving over more information. Many cyberthieves go after medical records because they often contain patients' Social Security numbers, birth dates, credit card numbers, and other personal data. Medical data theft has become an increasing concern as more health care providers switch from paper medical records to electronic ones.

There were more than 112 million health record breaches in the United States in 2015 alone. The top six breaches each affected at least 1 million individuals. In the largest single breach that year, hackers stole private information on about 78.8 million people when they broke into the computer system of the Anthem Blue Cross and Blue Shield medical insurance company.

Besides affecting victims emotionally and financially, these thefts have fueled widespread concerns about whether medical and government institutions can be trusted to protect citizens' personal information. "In 2015 more people than ever learned their data was stolen and used to target them in ways they could not have even imagined," explains cybersecurity expert Theresa Payton. "The consumer can't leave the safety of their data to any government or private sector entity. If someone has your data, it can and will be hacked unless you take your own steps to protect it."[28]

> "If someone has your data, it can and will be hacked unless you take your own steps to protect it."[28]
>
> —Theresa Payton, cybersecurity expert.

Medical Snoops and Thieves

Medical records breaches are not always conducted by high-tech hackers who live half a world away. Sometimes hospital employees are the ones who inappropriately access medical records. This is illegal under the federal Health Insurance Portability and Accountability Act (HIPAA), which mandates that medical providers keep patient records confidential. But either out of curiosity or for financial gain, hospital employees have breached the trust placed in them both by their patients and their industry. In one 2013 breach, for example, Cedars-Sinai Hospital in Los Angeles fired six workers for snooping in celebrity patients' hospital records. Among the records accessed were those belonging to actress Kim Kardashian after she gave birth to her daughter, North West.

Celebrities including Kim Kardashian (pictured in 2016) were targeted in a hospital data breach. Six employees of Cedars-Sinai Medical Center in Los Angeles were fired for snooping in celebrity medical records.

Murder by Hack

As of mid-2016, no one had been murdered as the result of some-one hacking into a computerized medical device—but security experts consider this to be a credible threat. Indeed, hackers could use a smartphone to remotely steal security codes and passwords. They could then use these to break into a computer-controlled hospital medical device or a wireless personal device like an insulin pump or pacemaker. In 2013, for example, security expert Jay Radcliffe, who uses an insulin pump to control his diabetes, showed attendees at a computer security conference how a hacker could reprogram the pump to deliver him a lethal dose of insulin.

Other experts have alerted medical care providers and government agencies to similar problems. For example, white-hat hacker Billy Rios, who helps companies improve computer security, demonstrated how a malicious hacker could easily hijack a hospital intravenous infusion pump and instruct it to administer a lethal dose of medication. Screen monitors at a nearby nursing station would not even detect such an event. "People that are connected to these devices are in a vulnerable state," says Rios. "They shouldn't have to worry about the cyber se-curity of the devices that are connected to them."

For years, most hospitals and government agencies ignored these reports because tampering had not actually occurred. But after nu-merous threat assessments, in 2015 the US Food and Drug Adminis-tration (FDA) began issuing advisories to hospitals about vulnerable medical equipment. The FDA also urges device manufacturers to up-grade security systems; the manufacturer is the only one that can in-stall new hardware and software to make these devices safer.

Quoted in Tammy Leitner, "Popular Hospital Medical Device Could Pose Hacking Threat," NBC Chicago, July 16, 2015. www.nbcchicago.com.

Other hospitals, particularly those in the Los Angeles area that serve many celebrities, have experienced similar data breaches. The University of California–Los Angeles Hospitals, for example, have been hit especially hard by employee-perpetrated data breaches. The most notorious breach occurred from 2004 to 2007, when administrative specialist Lawanda Jackson used her supervisor's password to access 939 patients' medical records, including those of pop star Britney Spears and actress Farrah Fawcett. Jackson then sold the records to the *National Enquirer*. After she was caught, Jackson lied to the *Los Angeles Times*, stating, "It was just me being nosy. . . . It wasn't for money or anything."[29] Evidence proved, however, that Jackson received money from the *National Enquirer* for the information. Although she faced fines of up to $250,000 and up to ten years in prison, Jackson died of cancer before the sentence could be imposed. The penalties for HIPAA violations are severe because patients and lawmakers consider medical records privacy to be extremely important.

In many cases employees who steal medical data are involved in more far-reaching identity theft schemes. Some predators steal from victims' bank accounts, abuse their credit cards, or open new credit card accounts using stolen information. Others take on the patient's identity to obtain medical care using the victim's medical insurance or sell the identity to others for this purpose. In one case a Howard University medical technician named Laurie Napper was caught selling patients' names, addresses, birth dates, and insurance information for $500 to $800 per file. She sold the information to criminals who posed as the patients to receive health care. Besides the financial and emotional damage done to victims, this type of identity theft causes the thief's medical information to appear in the victim's chart, which can lead to confusion and erroneous treatment. According to the World Privacy Forum, "Medical identity theft typically leaves a trail of falsified information in medical records that can plague victims' medical and financial lives for years."[30]

> "Medical identity theft typically leaves a trail of falsified information in medical records that can plague victims' medical and financial lives for years."[30]
>
> —The World Privacy Forum.

Medical Records Blackmail

Another type of medical records hacking involves blackmail. The first known instance of this occurred in 2003, after the University of California–San Francisco (UCSF) Medical Center hired a company called Transcription Stat to transcribe its medical records. Transcription involves transferring doctors' voice recordings about patient visits into electronic form. However, UCSF was unaware that Transcription Stat outsourced its work to a Pakistani woman named Lubna Baloch. Baloch sent UCSF an e-mail in which she threatened to post confidential patient records online unless the hospital paid her a ransom. UCSF paid the ransom to avoid a privacy scandal, then terminated its contract with Transcription Stat. But finding and prosecuting Baloch proved impossible, as happens in most cases that involve foreign predators.

Some hospitals and other medical providers do not back up their data, which leaves them vulnerable to a different kind of blackmail scheme in which thieves hijack data and demand a ransom to return it. In some cases organizations have had to pay the ransom in order to remain functional. In February 2016, for instance, after hackers stole data belonging to the Hollywood Presbyterian Medical Center, the center's CEO announced that paying the ransom of 40 bitcoins (about $16,664) was "the quickest and most efficient way to restore our systems and administrative functions."[31] In contrast, in 2012 Russian hackers took over the databases of the Miami Family Medicine Centre in Queensland, Australia, and demanded $4,000 for their return. However, the clinic had already backed up the data on a remote hard drive, so it did not pay the ransom.

Medical Device Hacking

Another type of electronic medical breach that concerns security experts is medical device hacking, in which predators breach computer systems that control medical monitoring and lifesaving devices in hospitals. Most high-tech medical equipment—including ventilators, intravenous pumps, and magnetic resonance imaging machines—is run by computers that are hooked

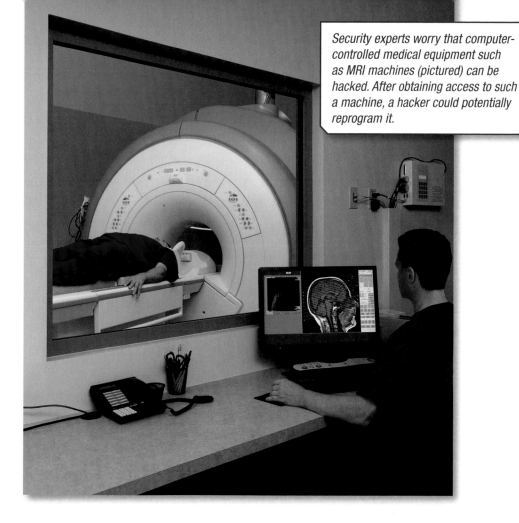

Security experts worry that computer-controlled medical equipment such as MRI machines (pictured) can be hacked. After obtaining access to such a machine, a hacker could potentially reprogram it.

up to a hospital's computer network. While this interconnectivity improves a device's functioning, it also makes it vulnerable to hacking. Once they have access, hackers could possibly reprogram the computers to alter treatment plans, withhold medication, or administer lethal doses of medication. Wireless personal medical devices like pacemakers and insulin pumps could also be vulnerable to cyberattacks, and the fear is that a predator might take control of the device and demand payment from the victim to release control. For this reason, the research and advisory firm Forrester named ransomware in medical devices as the single biggest cybersecurity threat for 2016.

As of mid-2016, there had been no known or documented case of anyone being held hostage or harmed via their medical device. But the fictional TV show *Homeland* depicted something like this, when a 2012 episode of the show featured terrorists who assassinated the vice president by hijacking his electronic pacemaker via smartphone and delivering a fatal shock to his heart. After the episode aired, numerous security consultants agreed that such a scenario could really happen. In fact, the threat of such a possibility was why former US vice president Dick Cheney insisted on having his doctors disable his pacemaker's wireless programming feature in 2007. After the *Homeland* episode aired, Cheney told *Daily Mail* reporters that it "was an accurate portrayal of what was possible."[32]

Insider Hacks

Sometimes, company insiders—people who work at a company—are the ones who hack personal information, records databases, or other systems. In fact, according to an IBM CyberSecurity Intelligence report, insiders are responsible for 55 percent of all data thefts of any kind. Of these insider attacks, 31.5 percent are malicious and 23.5 percent unintentional.

An unintentional breach may occur when an employee clicks on a phishing link in an infected e-mail. Although the employee probably means no harm, the damage that ensues can be significant. In fact, the 2015 Anthem breach resulted from employees clicking on phishing e-mails, which infected the entire computer network. Other times, employees may unknowingly use infected USB sticks (flash drives) or smartphone chargers to transfer malware. "The best way to get into an unprepared company is to sprinkle infected USB sticks with the company's logo around the car park," says cybersecurity expert Michael Goldsmith. "Some employee is bound to try one of them."[33] In 2012 hackers used this ploy to steal data from the Dutch chemical company DSM. A similar incident took place in 2013 when delegates at a G20 summit in Russia were given infected USB sticks and mobile phone chargers by their hosts, who apparently intended to use them to steal sensitive information.

On the other hand, inside employees might maliciously and intentionally steal data or personal information, sometimes because they hold a grudge against individual employees or the entire company. For example, Roger Duronio, an employee at UBS Wealth Management, was angry about not receiving a large bonus. He expressed his anger by damaging the company's computer system with malware. Other insiders may have financial motives, while some act on behalf of outside criminals who purchase data from them or befriend them and con them into revealing sensitive data. Whatever the motive, approximately 80 million insider cyberattacks take place in the United States annually, and these can be even more damaging than outsider attacks. According to cybersecurity experts David M. Upton and Sadie Creese, "Insiders can do much more serious harm than external hackers can, because they have much easier access to systems and a much greater window of opportunity."[34]

> "Insiders can do much more serious harm than external hackers can, because they have much easier access to systems and a much greater window of opportunity."[34]
>
> —David M. Upton and Sadie Creese, cybersecurity experts.

As with other types of cybercrimes, behavior experts have wondered whether the ease of tampering with digital technologies turns formerly moral employees into criminals. Most believe that usually, cyberhacking employees are already morally deficient individuals who probably would have been susceptible to corruption in pre-Internet times. Daniel Karson, chair of the information management and intelligence company Kroll, summed up the consensus by stating, "While technology has enabled new ways to perpetrate fraud, our daily work with clients confirms . . . that old fashioned theft, bribery and kickbacks are still amazingly effective and pervasive. Human nature being what it is, fraud will always be with us whether it occurs in a company's corner office or a world away in its supply chain."[35]

CHAPTER FOUR

Predators Can Be Peers

Some cyberpredators bully, taunt, or emotionally abuse others online. They are a significant concern, especially since their actions have led numerous young people to kill themselves. The US government's StopBullying.gov website states that cyberbullying includes posting messages, texts, photos, websites, or e-mails that are mean or embarrassing or transmit rumors.

Cyberbullies can be children, teenagers, or adults. About one-third of American teenagers and one in five Americans of all ages have been victims of cyberbullying. Although the problem gets a lot of attention, the Internet is still so relatively new that many laws and social conventions have not yet caught up with the technologies that allow people to publicly insult or harass others. Thus, as Alexis Moore and Laurie J. Edwards, authors of the book *Cyber Self-Defense*, point out, "If you destroy someone's life or reputation in the news media, you can be sued for defamation of character. If you do it online, you might get away with it."[36]

Free Speech or a Crime?

One reason many predators get away with online bullying is that heated controversies exist over whether cyberbullying constitutes free speech or criminal behavior. It can be difficult to distinguish between the right to speak freely and behavior that should be criminally liable for ruining reputations or driving people to commit suicide. For instance,

Tina Meier displays photos of her daughter Megan, who killed herself after relentless cyberbullying. The case inspired many communities to adopt laws that prohibit or punish cyberbullying.

consider the widely publicized 2006 case in which a thirteen-year-old girl named Megan Meier killed herself after being relentlessly cyberbullied by a forty-six-year-old woman named Lori Drew. Many people thought Drew should be prosecuted for murder, since her taunting and bullying drove Meier to suicide. However, Drew had never directly threatened Meier, and thus Drew's attorneys argued that she was just exercising her right to speak freely online. Drew was convicted of the much lesser crime of computer abuse and fraud, charges incurred because she pretended to be a sixteen-year-old boy while she tormented Meier.

Meier's case and ones like it led many localities to adopt new anti-cyberbullying laws, but some of these have been challenged or thrown out in court because they restrict freedom of expression. These were the issues at play in 2013 when lawmakers in Nova Scotia, Canada, passed a controversial law after relentless cyberbullying caused seventeen-year-old Rehtaeh Parsons to kill herself. The law forbade people from posting comments that hurt anyone's feelings and specified that violators could be sued, cut off from Internet access, and forbidden from communicating with an alleged victim. Opponents called the law "draconian,"[37] and in December 2015 the Supreme Court of Nova Scotia struck it down, arguing that it infringed on peoples' right to free expression. However, other laws have been criticized for being too lenient because they allow cyberpredators to post racist, sexist, or defamatory comments that would, if they were painted on a building or screamed in a school, be prosecuted as hate crimes.

Why Bully Others?

Amid the debates over the limits of free speech, cyberbullies continue to harass, threaten, terrorize, and stalk others. Their reasons for doing so vary; cyberbullies are spurned lovers, jealous coworkers or students, angry neighbors, resentful clique rivals, and mentally ill sociopaths. Some cyberbullies bully others just to have fun. But no matter what the bully's motivation may be, the consequences to victims can be devastating.

Online bullies are often angry, insecure individuals who intimidate, terrorize, and physically or emotionally abuse others offline, too. These individuals seem to lack self-restraint and cannot stop themselves from lashing out. In other cases the anonymity of cyberspace and the lack of significant consequences for cyberbullying can push individuals who restrain themselves offline to lash out online. "Anonymity may drive more deviant behavior, because it is easy to avoid consequences," writes Ohio State University psychology professor Jesse Fox. "It is also easier to type something offensive or mean into a screen than to say it to someone's face."[38] Sometimes, this quality—known as online disinhibition—

Cyberbullying and Its Consequences

On September 22, 2012, eighteen-year-old Tyler Clementi killed himself by jumping off the George Washington Bridge, which connects New York with New Jersey. He did this after experiencing online harassment and bullying at the hands of Dharun Ravi, his roommate at Rutgers University. The case triggered widespread outrage not only because it involved the suicide of a young person who was cyberbullied, but also because Clementi was gay and the cyberbullying was ruled a hate crime.

The roommates had little in common and barely spoke. But Ravi secretly set up a webcam to record Clementi while Clementi was alone with another male in the dorm room. Ravi then watched the camera feed from his friend Molly Wei's computer. After Ravi and Wei saw Clementi embracing his male friend, Ravi tweeted, "I saw him making out with a dude. Yay." Ravi then hosted an online viewing party for friends. He planned to do this again after Clementi's next encounter, but Clementi unplugged Ravi's computer after spotting the webcam.

Clementi read Ravi's Twitter feed and was humiliated. He requested a single room on September 21 but killed himself before one could be assigned to him. Afterward, Ravi claimed he was not homophobic, but just a boisterous, arrogant teenager who enjoyed poking fun at others. Anil Kappa, a friend of Ravi's father, described Ravi's actions as simply "a kid's prank that went wrong." Nonetheless, in 2012 Ravi was convicted of invasion of privacy, bias intimidation, and other charges.

Quoted in Ian Parker, "The Story of a Suicide," *New Yorker*, February 6, 2012. www.new yorker.com.

occurs because an individual is indifferent to the fact that there is a real person on the receiving end of his or her abuse. Indeed, numerous studies indicate that the ease of communicating via cell phone, text, e-mail, and instant messaging has led many people to avoid face-to-face interactions with others. One study at the University of Delaware, for example, found that 47.3 percent of college students surveyed admitted that they use some form of electronic messaging to avoid directly speaking to people face-to-face or on the telephone. This can lead to a diminished ability to understand or care about peoples' reactions.

Psychologists believe that many vicious or obscene comments made by cyberbullies—particularly young ones—also result from a bully's need to be noticed. They might also result from feeling jealous of peers who receive in-person attention or online notoriety via viral posts. Paula Todd, author of the book *Extreme Mean*, explains that "mean and menacing comments . . . can temporarily shift a shaft of limelight to the viewer who feels like an outsider."[39]

Studies indicate that people who crave attention and feel unimportant are especially likely to become cyberbullies, because making others look bad helps them feel better about themselves. This was one of many findings by criminology researchers Justin W. Patchin and Sameer Hinduja, founders and directors of the Cyberbullying Research Center. Patchin and Hinduja have found that middle school students who experience stress, anger, depression, or frustration about their lives are also likely to cyberbully. Some who do this are unaware that their actions hurt their victims, while others do not care. For instance, when twelve-year-old Rebecca Sedwick of Lakeland, Florida, killed herself in 2013 after she was relentlessly cyberbullied by classmates Katelyn Roman and Guadalupe Shaw, Shaw wrote, "Yes ik (I know) I bullied REBECCA nd she killed her self but IDGAF (I don't give a f—k)."[40]

Law enforcement and behavior experts find the amount of venomous and obscene online taunting of victims and their families—even after a victim has died—to be especially disturbing. For example, after seventh-grader Mitchell Henderson killed himself after being cyberbullied, his grieving parents received countless harassing and hurtful phone calls and e-mails. One message stated, "Hi, this is Mitchell, I'm at the cemetery."[41] In a different

> "Mean and menacing comments . . . can temporarily shift a shaft of limelight to the viewer who feels like an outsider."[39]
>
> —Investigative writer Paula Todd, author of the book *Extreme Mean.*

case Carol Todd—the mother of Amanda Todd, who killed her-self because a cyberpredator posted nude photos of her online—received thousands of online threats and insults after Amanda's death. "It's all your fault your daughter died," stated one particu-larly hurtful message. "Why the f*** didn't you take away your whore daughters webcam. . . . Go kill yourself."[42] No one really knows why people—young or old—treat others this way, espe-cially someone enduring the unspeakable grief of losing a child. But Patchin, Hinduja, and other experts suggest it is a combina-tion of factors that range from insecurity, to anger, to a decline in social values, to the way in which machines have obscured the humanity of their users.

Cyberbullying on Social Media and Gaming Sites

Social media and gaming websites are often criticized for doing little or nothing to stop the cyberbullying that proliferates among their pages and forums. Rafi Fine, who coproduces the YouTube interview show *Kids React*, argues that these sites "do nothing, they just put up a button that says 'report' and then when you ac-tually report, nothing is done whatsoever."[43] This is partly because website administrators hesitate to restrict free speech, and partly because it is an overwhelming task to track and remove millions of venomous posts. For example, many players have complained that the online game *World of Warcraft* has few or no conse-quences for bullying others. *World of Warcraft* administrators, however, stress that subscribers are expected to adhere to a no-bullying policy—but they state that with millions of subscribers, it is impossible to police and ban all such posts.

The term *griefers* is commonly used to refer to online game players who harass and threaten other players. Griefers often bul-ly others on massively multiplayer online role-playing games such as *World of Warcraft* or even single-player games like *Minecraft*. The Michigan State University New Bullying project describes griefers in the following way: "Griefers don't play by the rules and attempt to cause as much distress and discomfort for other play-ers as possible."[44]

Griefers achieve their goals in different ways in different situations. For example, in *Minecraft*, players spend many hours, weeks, or even months building structures and machines. However, griefers can hack into other players' accounts and destroy their creations in a split second. Even when players employ protective software, griefers devise ways to trick the system and make themselves site administrators, which gives them access to other players' accounts. In other situations griefers steal other players' passwords. They then use them to hack into their accounts and send harassing messages under their victim's name, for which the victims are then blamed. Some griefers even post private messages with virus-infected links to try to disable other players' computers.

Often, a griefer's goal is to force a particular gamer to leave the game; however, based on remarks by psychologist Mike Ambinder, an article on the Michigan State University New Bullying Project website concludes that "many people get pleasure from griefing others, and it often becomes a competition to see who can cause the most chaos."[45] The phenomenon of joining com-

Griefers hack into other players' accounts and wreak havoc in online games. In the game Minecraft, they often destroy the structures and machines a player has built. Griefers sometimes even get their victims to leave the game entirely.

Personality Traits of Online Predators

A 2014 study by University of Manitoba psychology professor Erin Buckels and her colleagues explored the often-asked question of why online bullies and other trolls do what they do. These researchers assessed the relationship between what is known as the Dark Tetrad of personality and online behavior. The Dark Tetrad describes the personality traits of people who tend to be the worst kinds of criminals and predators. These individuals are usually narcissists (completely selfish), psychopaths (born with no conscience), and sadists (enjoy hurting others).

The study found that online trolls who most enjoy what they do rate highest on the trait of sadism. Those who derive less pleasure from hurting others rate lower on sadism and higher on other traits. The researchers thus concluded that sadists, in particular, prey on people online mostly because they enjoy hurting others. "Trolls and sadists feel sadistic glee at the distress of others," they wrote. "Sadists just want to have fun . . . and the Internet is their playground!" While not all cyberbullies are sadists, this study indicates that the ones who truly enjoy bullying others—like gaming griefers—are ones whom psychologists define as having sadistic traits.

The researchers also explored whether Internet technologies tend to turn otherwise nice people into predators. They concluded that people who are already bad use the Internet in bad ways because "antisocial individuals have greater opportunities to connect with similar others, and to pursue their personal brand of 'self expression' than they did before the advent of the Internet."

Erin Buckels et al., "Trolls Just Want to Have Fun," *Personality and Individual Differences*, 2014. http://www.sciencedirect.com/science/article/pii/S0191886914000324.

petitive griefing bouts to compound the effects of bullying is an example of what psychologists call the mob mentality. "The more players are engaged in destructive behaviors, the more likely others are to join in,"[46] the same article explains.

Mob Mentality

The mob mentality is partly responsible for making griefing and other types of cyberbullying so pervasive and for allowing it to spiral out of control. Psychologist Wendy James writes that the mob mentality functions as a specialized type of disinhibition. "What we might not do as individuals we may do as part of a group," she explains. "People may lose control of their usual inhibitions, as their mentality becomes that of the group."[47]

Experts say that the innocent bystanders who "like" or share cyberbullies' postings are in reality not so innocent. Even though they may not have written an offensive post, they are complicit in perpetuating and intensifying the negative effects on victims. "The bystander is the invisible engine in the cycle of bullying," explains Jonathan Cohen, author of the book *Caring Classrooms/Intelligent Schools*. "The nature of the bully-victim interaction . . . is shaped and maintained by the demand of the audience of bystanders."[48]

A study published in 2013 by the Pew Research Center shows that up to 95 percent of teens who use social media report that they have witnessed cruel cyberbullying behavior that no one challenges or criticizes. Many who go along with or encourage cyberbullies do so because they do not want to be seen as outsiders or as uncool. But antibullying activists say that ignoring or challenging a bully is often the best way to stop him or her. "Sometimes all it takes is for one person to say 'No' or 'Stop,'" write Moore and Edwards in *Cyber Self-Defense*. "When one person has the courage to declare 'Enough,' others who have been afraid to speak up will follow that lead."[49]

Sometimes, cyberbullying victims muster the courage to overcome cyberpredators, even in the face of a mob. In 2011 seventeen-year-old cyberbullying victim Nicole Edgington and her mother, Shawn, started the Great American NO BULL Challenge to combat cyberbullying. Nicole endured years of abusive and ter-

> "What we might not do as individuals we may do as part of a group. People may lose control of their usual inhibitions, as their mentality becomes that of the group."[47]
>
> —Psychologist Wendy James.

rifying electronic threats because several students at her school mistakenly believed she had turned them in for being drunk on campus. Denying the accusations only intensified the bullying, so Nicole deleted her Facebook account and ignored the abusive texts she received. She began speaking about cyberbullying at schools and took pride in helping other victims overcome their situation. Although many people continued to harass her via text, Nicole was gratified when her actions led one person who had previously tormented her to apologize.

Effects on Victims

Whether victims or bystanders challenge cyberbullies, taking a stance can diminish bullying's devastating effects. For one, it lets a victim know the whole world is not against him or her. Indeed, much of the trauma that victims experience results from watching hundreds, even thousands, of bystanders share abusive messages or click that they like the messages. Studies indicate that most victims consider cyberbullying to be worse than in-person bullying, in part because countless numbers of people can participate. The other devastating thing about cyberbullying is that it can occur 24/7. As Kate McHugh, who experienced both in-person and online bullying in middle and high school, stated, "No matter how much I was battered at school, I could always run home to the quiet of my own room. The way those mean kids used the Internet took away any kind of escape for me."[50]

Because of this, victims of cyberbullying are more likely to contemplate or attempt suicide than victims of in-person bullying, according to a 2014 study reported in *JAMA Pediatrics*. Naturally, not all victims try to kill themselves. But many experience long-term emotional trauma and critical disruptions in their lifestyle. For example, many victims become withdrawn and avoid going to school or social events. Many avoid using digital devices, have trouble sleeping, and develop eating disorders. Cyberbullying also leads to or worsens depression and other crippling psychological disorders in many victims, along with provoking self-harm and substance abuse.

Victims of cyberpredators have also lost their jobs or friends after the predator bombards coworkers or friends with e-mails and other messages that berate the victim. In one case a real estate agent named Nico suffered severe emotional and professional harm after a coworker named Brooklyn retaliated against him for rejecting her sexual advances. Brooklyn posted anonymous unflattering comments about him on social media sites and business-rating sites and also concocted stories about how he sexually assaulted her. This cost Nico many clients, friends, and eventually, his job.

For some victims, the only way to escape the torment is to move far away and start over. Victims who receive death threats from a vengeful or demented cyberpredator may even have to cut all ties with family and friends to leave a former life behind and assume a new identity in a witness-protection program. But even with a new identity, some live in constant fear that the predator will track them down. In such instances the same Internet that allows fast, easy communications and interactions worldwide becomes an instrument of terror for cyberbullying victims.

CHAPTER FIVE

Combating Online Predators

The proliferation of online predators and the damage they cause has led to a pressing need for ways to combat this growing and ever-evolving challenge. In fact, a 2015 national security report revealed that the FBI considers cybercrime to be the most serious type of crime the United States currently faces. Several government agencies are thus actively combating cyberpredators by educating the public, cooperating with local and international law enforcement agencies, and aggressively prosecuting offenders.

Agencies involved in combating cyberpredators include the US Department of Health and Human Services Office for Civil Rights (OCR), the FBI, and the US Department of Homeland Security. The OCR is responsible for enforcing HIPAA laws and investigating and prosecuting medical data thieves and those who commit health-related cybercrimes. The FBI investigates and works with local law enforcement agencies to prosecute cybercriminals engaged in identity theft, cyberterrorism, espionage, ransomware, fraud, and crimes against children. The Department of Homeland Security oversees the US Secret Service and the US Immigration and Customs Enforcement (ICE) agencies, which each have several divisions that train law enforcement personnel to combat cybercrimes, track and arrest online criminals worldwide, and operate computer forensics laboratories.

Computer Forensics

Computer forensics laboratories specialize in examining and analyzing digital data and thus play a huge role in fighting cybercrime. Texts, photos, phone calls, Internet search data, and smartphones' Global Positioning System (GPS) data can tell investigators a lot about how an online predator planned and executed a crime. For example, if a cell phone user texted someone to arrange a meeting, forensics experts can retrieve these texts and learn about where the parties plan to be. GPS locators offer further information about when and where the phone user was located at a particular time. In addition, Internet search data can reveal that an individual researched a particular bank's policies, for example, prior to hacking the bank's website. Forensics teams can find this information even if someone has deleted files or a search history. This is because digital information remains on a computer's hard drive or mobile device's SIM (subscriber identity module) card.

One area in which computer forensics has been extremely valuable is in catching and prosecuting online sexual predators. The Department of Homeland Security's Child Exploitation Investigations Unit operates high-tech forensics laboratories that help its own agents and law enforcement personnel all over the world solve cases. Forensics agents work with case agents, who are traditional detectives, to achieve their goals. In 2014 the unit arrested more than two thousand pedophiles.

One case led ICE forensics agents to Puerto Rico after a forensics detective in Texas uncovered a child pornography ring that sold access to photos and videos through an online subscription service. The detective obtained the subscriber list, and ICE agents used it to pursue subscribers who purchased large amounts of child porn. Their investigation led them to a home in Aguadilla, Puerto Rico, where two adult brothers, Joseph and Emmanuel, lived with their parents. The agents seized three computers and found large amounts of child pornography on the computer belonging to the brother named Joseph. Joseph claimed his brother Emmanuel had placed the pornography there. But one agent analyzed the distinctive ways in which each brother organized and

The federal government operates computer forensics laboratories aimed at helping law enforcement personnel track down online predators. The US Immigration and Customs Enforcement Cyber Crimes Center in Virginia (pictured) operates one such lab.

labeled his computer files. Joseph's files were neatly arranged and labeled like the pornography files were; Emmanuel's were not. The agent was thus able to prove that Joseph placed the pornography on his own computer.

Another way in which forensics agents find cybercriminals is by tracking Internet protocol (IP) addresses. An IP address is a unique number that identifies the computer from which messages or photos were sent. This address can provide clues about a predator's physical address. In one case Australian police contacted the Department of Homeland Security's Computer Forensics Unit after arresting a couple for child pornography. A photo on the couple's computer that showed an adult molesting a child had been sent from an e-mail address in the United States. US agents served a search warrant on the e-mail service provider, which forced the company to identify the IP address associated with that particular e-mail address. The agents traced the IP address to a woman in Pennsylvania. Agents in Philadelphia obtained a search warrant, went to the woman's house, and discovered that her daughter

It Started with a Sunflower Sign

The Department of Homeland Security's Victim Identification Program (VIP), headquartered at the Cyber Crimes Center in Washington, DC, has helped solve thousands of crimes involving sexual predators. Investigators use advanced image-enhancing technologies to analyze details in the background of online photos to help identify victims. In the first case VIP investigators worked after the program was established in 2011, agents noticed a blurred road sign with a sunflower in a photo of a young female victim that a pedophile had posted online. After researching, they concluded the photo was taken somewhere in Kansas, based on information about a unique sunflower graphic the state of Kansas uses on some of its road signs. A team of agents drove around Kansas for two weeks and finally found the road on which the sign in the photo was located. With the help of local police, the agents found the house on that road in which the victim lived. The victim identified the pedophile, and police arrested him.

One year after the successful conclusion of this case, the VIP unit commemorated its anniversary by starting an operation it called Operation Sunflower. It lasted from November 1 to December 7, 2012. During this operation, the team identified 123 sexual abuse victims in the United States and abroad who ranged in age from toddlers to adolescents. Identifying these victims led to the arrest of 245 pedophiles in nineteen US states. Since then, the VIP team has identified thousands more victims.

was the girl in the photo. The woman's boyfriend had molested the child while the woman took photos. Both were arrested.

Reeling In Sexual Predators

Sometimes, tracing an IP address is impossible because predators often use software like Tor, which masks IP addresses by sending computer messages on a convoluted path across the world via the dark web. The dark web consists of computer networks that are hidden from the search engines most people use. In such instances agents have to use other techniques to find sexual predators. They sometimes use a technique called victim identification. The ICE's Victim Identification Program uses image-enhancing technologies to analyze digital photos for clues that help identify victims. As investigator Jim Cole told NBC10.com, "We're not really looking at the abuse of the victim as much as we're looking at things in the background. We look at logos, products, personalized items. Sometimes there have been certificates from schools and trophies, uniforms from different things like Boy Scouts."[51] These details are especially useful for identifying victims who are molested in their own homes. Image-enhancing techniques have helped Victim Identification Program investigators find thousands of sexual predators.

Other law enforcement agents use methods like posing as underage children to locate sexual cyberpredators. In one investigation, FBI special agent Michael Whitmire, who works with the FBI's Houston Area Child Exploitation Task Force, pretended to be a thirteen-year-old girl on an Internet teen chat site. Within minutes of posting, the "girl" was participating in eight different conversations with sexual predators, who asked questions such as, "How tall are you baby?" and "Still a virgin?"[52]

Undercover agents like Whitmire learn to chat like teenagers to convincingly play their roles. For example, Whitmire used teen-speak like "where ru" and "yuck"[53] when he typed messages in the chat. Whitmire was also careful not to entrap suspects by initiating sex-related conversations. It is much easier to convict a predator of soliciting sex with a minor when the predator is the one who broaches the subject. Otherwise, the predator could claim in court that the detective was the one who started a sexual conversation. This particular chat scenario led Whitmire to obtain enough evidence to have at least one pedophile arrested. Similar investigations by Whitmire and other agents at this facility have played a role in the arrests of hundreds of sexual predators.

Another group that goes undercover to combat sexual predators consists of white-hat hackers. Many set up fake social media accounts and pretend to be a young girl or boy. One such hacker revealed in 2014 that he electronically lured and exposed at least twenty online sexual predators each day. When a pedophile takes the bait, the hacker either immediately notifies police or informs the pedophile that police will be notified unless he or she stops victimizing children.

Educating the Public

While cyberdetectives and high-tech methods of finding online predators are critical in fighting Internet criminals, security experts emphasize that computer users play an equally important role. "Cybersecurity is a shared responsibility" is the main message of the Department of Homeland Security's Stop.Think.Connect. Campaign. The campaign's website states, "We each have to do our part to keep the Internet safe."[54] This is why law enforcement and child welfare agencies work to educate the public and why specific programs are directed at parents. Parents are encouraged to discuss the risks of going online with their children. For instance, in 2007 the National Center for Missing & Exploited Children started the Take 25 initiative to encourage parents to take twenty-five minutes to talk to their kids about Internet safety.

> "Cybersecurity is a shared responsibility. We each have to do our part to keep the Internet safe."[54]
>
> —The US Department of Homeland Security's Stop.Think.Connect. Campaign.

The FBI's parent-education programs emphasize that parents should also monitor their children's online activities. Some parents put filtering software on their computers to prevent their children from visiting certain types of websites, but most parents do not monitor their kids' online use. The 2013 McAfee Digital Deception Study found that only 20 percent of parents say they know how to monitor their children's online activities, and 77 percent say they do not have the time or energy to do so. "Parents need to have their kids' passwords to their Facebook pages, to their phones," says FBI media representative Amy Thoreson. "They need to inspect the phones. Kids are doing things 'cause kids will be kids and they don't think it will involve a stranger."[55]

Parent education programs urge parents to monitor their kids' online activities. These programs also suggest greater vigilance in checking cell phones that kids use.

Dos and Don'ts

Law enforcement agencies have also launched campaigns to increase awareness of practices that reduce or increase vulnerability to cyberpredators. Installing and regularly updating good antimalware software, choosing strong passwords, not clicking on links or opening suspicious-looking e-mails, and not friending strangers are a few of the precautions that reduce the chances of being victimized.

Preparing for a New Type of Warfare

The world's nations have long kept armies and employed other defensive techniques to protect themselves from outside invaders. But in the digital age, nations need to prepare for a new type of warfare: cyberinvasions.

As of 2016, the largest scale cyberinvasion was a 2007 attack that shut down the Estonian government. Russian nationalists, upset by the Estonian government's relocation of a statue that honored Russians killed in World War II, encouraged Russians everywhere to flood Estonian websites with traffic. Hackers also infected millions of computers worldwide with malware that forced these computers to participate in the attack. Thus, websites that normally received about one thousand visits per day crashed after receiving two thousand visits per second. As a result, the Estonian government and economy were completely shut down. The Estonian government believes, but never proved, that the Russian government orchestrated the attack. Whether or not this is true, national security experts have stated that launching an untraceable cyberattack rather than physically invading Estonia was a smart way to do damage without provoking a military response from the North Atlantic Treaty Organization (NATO) nations, with which Estonia is allied.

The attack highlighted that preparing for and countering cyberattacks require the same strategic planning and cooperation among nations as traditional war readiness. Indeed, after the attack, Germany, Finland, Slovenia, Israel, and NATO helped the Estonian Computer Emergency Response team restore computer operations. Estonia's European allies also established international networks of experts who can give immediate assistance if similar crises arise elsewhere.

On the other hand, oversharing personal information vastly increases one's chance of becoming a cyberpredator's victim. Many of the seemingly innocuous bits of information that people post on social media can give cyberpredators all the data they need to steal money or find a potential sexual abuse victim. For example, the Experian credit monitoring service ProtectMyID cautions that posting seemingly harmless details—like a dog's name or the name of a school's sports team—gives cyberthieves hints about individuals' passwords or answers to security questions that might be used to verify a bank account. Posting a birth date can be risky for similar reasons.

Law enforcement agencies also see many cases in which social media postings lead thieves right to peoples' homes. In one case in Arkansas, this happened after an Instagram user boasted about and shared a photo of a Christmas gift. The photo contained a geotag—a piece of data that indicates where and when the photo was taken. Thieves were essentially given a roadmap to the person's house. In another case an Australian teen posted photos of herself counting large wads of cash with her grandmother. Thieves later showed up to look for the cash.

Commonsense security measures and education are also important to curb both accidental and deliberate insider hacks in business and institutional settings. Security experts advise companies to implement training programs that teach employees to watch out for suspicious e-mails and websites. Some employers also forbid the personal use of company computers. However, some security experts suggest using an opposite tactic. For instance, Oxford University cybersecurity experts David M. Upton and Sadie Creese believe that employers should allow employees to go wherever they want to online. At the same time, they encourage employers to regularly monitor all employees' Internet use and to perform psychological assessments and observations to determine which employees pose hacking and sabotage risks.

Legal Measures

Another tool against online predators is the law. Numerous new or amended federal, state, and local laws have been introduced to combat various types of online crimes, including financial scams, medical records breaches, and cyberbullying.

While no federal antibullying statute yet exists, many schools and localities have established strict policies and laws that set forth serious consequences for offenders. Sometimes, however, it is difficult to prosecute cyberbullies because the distinction between free speech and criminal behavior can be unclear. When online predators make direct threats, they are almost always prosecuted. But merely stating that someone is, for example, ugly and should kill herself is not necessarily viewed as illegal. Some US states have tried to address this dilemma by clearly defining what constitutes unlawful online behavior. New York state laws, for example, specify online harassment, bullying, intimidation, taunting, and discrimination as unlawful and subject to punishment.

However, numerous psychologists and law enforcement experts caution that even though bullying should not be tolerated, it is important not to overreact by prosecuting and placing every child who cyberbullies into the criminal justice system. As criminologist Justin W. Patchin writes, "The vast majority of cyberbullying incidents can and should be handled informally: with parents, schools, and others working together to address the problem before it rises to the level of a violation of criminal law."[56]

In an effort to stem the onslaught of medical records breaches, some states have passed laws that require health care providers to implement computer security software and to educate their employees about the importance of data security. For example, a New Jersey law passed in 2015 requires all medical insurance companies and health care providers to encrypt all personal information. Federal HIPAA laws have also been amended to require health care providers and others to strengthen their computer security with enhanced protective software and employee edu-

> "The vast majority of cyberbullying incidents can and should be handled informally: with parents, schools, and others working together to address the problem before it rises to the level of a violation of criminal law."[56]
>
> —Criminologist Justin W. Patchin of the Cyberbullying Research Center.

cation and training programs. The OCR, which enforces HIPAA laws, may impose fines and other penalties on health care institutions that lack adequate computer security. For instance, in December 2015 the OCR fined University of Washington Medicine $750,000 and mandated that it institute an employee education and computer security plan to correct weaknesses that led to the theft of about ninety thousand patients' health records.

Debates About Ending Online Anonymity

Another type of legal change that has been suggested is ending online anonymity, which fuels many crimes. This idea is extremely controversial. People who favor ending online anonymity argue that it would allow police to easily trace criminal activities back to the perpetrators. For example, in 2014 the British Parliament's House of Lords issued a report that endorsed this position. "There is little point in criminalising certain behaviour and at the same time legitimately making that same behaviour impossible to detect,"[57] the report noted. But Mike Masnick, editor of the *Techdirt* blog, argues against this viewpoint by pointing out that cyberdetectives can and do find anonymous criminals. He also stated that in the nondigital world, "anyone can walk into a store or a bank and hold it up. And they can do it without identifying themselves at the door."[58]

Other debates about ending online anonymity center on free speech issues and on protecting political dissidents or people who must remain anonymous (such as domestic violence victims). Such issues led to the defeat of a New York law proposed in 2012 that would have forced website administrators to remove anonymous comments. Indeed, numerous legal experts have argued that restricting online anonymity would be unconstitutional in the United States. According to attorney Kurt Opsahl, for example, "The right to speak anonymously is part of the First Amendment and has been since the founding of this country."[59] However, frustration over thousands of anonymous vile, uncivilized comments has led some media outlets either to ban anonymous comments or to completely

THE
HUFFINGTON
POST

The online news site Huffington Post is one of the media organizations that has banned the posting of anonymous comments. This represents an effort to eliminate the prevalence of nasty comments that are often posted anonymously.

do away with online comment sections. ESPN, the *Huffington Post*, and *Popular Science* are examples of sites that have banned the posting of anonymous comments.

Several US states have bypassed free speech arguments and passed laws that only restrict certain types of anonymous postings. In 2015, for example, Florida passed a law that prohibits anonymously posting anything that has audio or audiovisual elements. This law aims to stop people from posting pirated music or videos. Tennessee has a similar law, and one was proposed in California in 2015.

Challenges Ahead

Addressing the security risks posed by all types of cyberpredators and dealing with the damage they leave in their wake presents ongoing challenges. But even though the Internet gives predators new ways to network and commit crimes, it also gives law enforcement agencies new ways to track these criminals. While cyberpredators devise new ways to inflict terror and damage, equally dedicated individuals and teams of law enforcement and victims' advocacy specialists spend their lives fighting online predators and bringing them to justice. As one agent with the Department of Homeland Security's Child Exploitation Investigations Unit put it, "We never give up the fight, we never give up trying to find a child who's being abused . . . [even though] it's like putting your finger in a dam."[60]

At the very least, dedicated cybercrime fighters hope that each individual who combats cybercriminals and uses online technologies for good can help tip the balance to make the Internet more like its founders intended. The British computer scientist Tim Berners-Lee, who invented the World Wide Web in 1989, once stated that his intention was "to foster creative interconnectivity, in which people from all around the world can build something together."[61] Whether that something is good or bad depends on the people who use the Internet, not on the Internet itself.

> "There is little point in criminalising certain behaviour and at the same time legitimately making that same behaviour impossible to detect."[57]
>
> —A 2014 report issued by the British Parliament's House of Lords on why Internet activity should not be anonymous.

SOURCE NOTES

Introduction: The Dark Side of the Internet

1. Merriam-Webster, "Predator." www.merriam-webster.com.
2. Quoted in Federal Bureau of Investigation, "Testimony," December 10, 2014. www.fbi.gov.
3. Quoted in Kristin Finklea and Catherine A. Theohary, "Cybercrime: Conceptual Issues for Congress and U.S. Law Enforcement," Congressional Research Service, January 15, 2015. www.fas.org.
4. Gary Small, "Is the Internet Killing Empathy?," *Small's Blog*, January 8, 2013. ww.drgarysmall.com.
5. Azy Barak, ed., *Psychological Aspects of Cyberspace: Theory, Research, Applications*. Cambridge: Cambridge University Press, 2008, p. 129.
6. Eric Schmidt and Jared Cohen, *The New Digital Age*. New York: Knopf, 2013, p. 3.

Chapter One: The Threat from Sexual Predators

7. Quoted in Danya Bacchus, "FBI Gives Inside Look at World of Online Predators," NBC 7 San Diego, November 16, 2013. www.nbcsandiego.com.
8. Federal Bureau of Investigation, "Child Predators," May 17, 2011. www.fbi.gov.
9. Federal Bureau of Investigation, "Child Predators."
10. Ann Brenoff, "The 12 Apps That Every Parent of a Teen Should Know About," *Huffington Post*, February 17, 2016. www.huffingtonpost.com.
11. Quoted in Alexandra Carlton, "Convicted Sex Offender's Chilling Account of Grooming Children," Kidspot, February 4, 2016. www.kidspot.com.au.
12. Quoted in Deborah Amos, "Online with a Sexual Predator," ABC News, August 14, 2014. http://abcnews.go.com.
13. Quoted in Amos, "Online with a Sexual Predator."
14. Quoted in CBS News Crimesider Staff, "FBI Seeks 240 Victims of Man Imprisoned for Sextortion," CBS News, July 8, 2015. www.cbsnews.com.
15. Kristen Schweizer, "Pedophiles Lured by Avatar in Tech Industry Porn Fight," Bloomberg Technology, April 16, 2014. www.bloomberg.com.

16. Quoted in Schweizer, "Pedophiles Lured by Avatar in Tech Industry Porn Fight."
17. Quoted in Kelly Mclaughlin, "'He Ruined My Life': Victims Reveal How They Were Left Suicidal After Their Naked Photos Were Posted Online by 'Revenge Porn' Mastermind as He's Finally Jailed for 18 Years," *Daily Mail* (London), April 4, 2015. www.dailymail.co.uk.
18. Quoted in CBS News Crimesider Staff, "FBI Seeks 240 Victims of Man Imprisoned for Sextortion."

Chapter Two: Tricks and Technologies Used by Online Predators

19. Bureau of Justice Statistics, "Identity Theft," May 28, 2016. www.bjs.gov.
20. Federal Bureau of Investigation, "Cyber Crime." www.fbi.gov.
21. Quoted in Michael Seese, *Scrappy Information Security*. Cupertino, CA: Scrappy About, 2009, p. 117.
22. Quoted in Seese, *Scrappy Information Security*, p. 117.
23. Quoted in Conference of Defence Associations Institute, "Cyber Attacks: Waking Up to the Threat," June 19, 2015. www.cdainstitute.ca.
24. Robert Siciliano, "What Is a Keylogger?," *McAfee Consumer Blog*, July 23, 2013. https://blogs.mcafee.com.
25. Quoted in Alexis Moore and Laurie J. Edwards, *Cyber Self-Defense*. Guilford, CT: Lyons, 2014, p. 50.

Chapter Three: Data Breaches and Identity Theft

26. Alexis A. Moore, "'I Was a Victim of Cyberstalking'—One Woman's Story," About News, 2016. http://womensissues.about.com.
27. Quoted in Cook County Recorder of Deeds, "CCRD Fraud Unit Work Leads to Alleged Scammer's Arrest." http://cookrecorder.com.
28. Quoted in Dan Munro, "Data Breaches in Healthcare Totaled over 112 Million Records in 2015," *Forbes*, December 31, 2015. www.forbes.com.
29. Quoted in Charles Ornstein, "Just 'Nosy,' Says Figure in Medical Data Scandal," *Los Angeles Times*, April 9, 2008. http://articles.latimes.com.
30. World Privacy Forum, "Medical Identity Theft." www.worldprivacyforum.org.
31. Quoted in Fox News, "Hospital Pays Nearly $17G in Bitcoins to Hackers Who Disabled Computer Network," February 18, 2016. www.foxnews.com.

32. Quoted in *Daily Mail* (London), "Dick Cheney Reveals He Feared Terrorists Would Kill Him by Staging Homeland-Style Attack on His Pacemaker," October 18, 2013. www.dailymail.co.uk.

33. Quoted in David M. Upton and Sadie Creese, "The Danger from Within," *Harvard Business Review*, September 2014. https://hbr.org.

34. Upton and Creese, "The Danger from Within."

35. Quoted in Business Wire, "The Threat Within: Insider Fraud on the Rise," November 23, 2015. www.businesswire.com.

Chapter Four: Predators Can Be Peers

36. Moore and Edwards, *Cyber Self-Defense*, p. ix.

37. Brett Ruskin, "Court Strikes Down Anti-cyberbullying Law Created After Rehtaeh Parson's Death," CBC News, December 11, 2015. www.cbc.ca.

38. Jesse Fox, "Why the Online Trolls Troll," *Psychology Today*, August 12, 2014. www.psychologytoday.com.

39. Paula Todd, *Extreme Mean*. Toronto: McClelland & Stewart, 2014, p. 68.

40. Quoted in Stephen Rex Brown, "Florida Teen Cleared of Cyberbullying Rebecca Sedwick to Suicide: 'I Did Nothing Wrong,'" *New York Daily News*, November 21, 2013. www.nydailynews.com.

41. Quoted in Mattathias Schwartz, "The Trolls Among Us," *New York Times*, August 3, 2008. www.nytimes.com.

42. Quoted in Todd, *Extreme Mean*, pp. 14–15.

43. Quoted in Todd, *Extreme Mean*, p. 72.

44. Dmitri Barvinok, "Bullies in Video Games: Griefers," Michigan State University School of Journalism, February 5, 2012. http://news.jrn.msu.edu.

45. Barvinok, "Bullies in Video Games."

46. Barvinok, "Bullies in Video Games."

47. Wendy James, "The Psychology of Mob Mentality and Violence," Dr. Wendy James, Ph.D., July 18, 2013. www.drwendyjames.com.

48. Jonathan Cohen, *Caring Classrooms/Intelligent Schools: The Social Emotional Education of Young Children*. New York: Teachers College, 2001, p. 9.

49. Moore and Edwards, *Cyber Self-Defense*, pp. 170–71.

50. Quoted in Todd, *Extreme Mean*, p. 131.

Chapter Five: Combating Online Predators

51. Quoted in Vince Lattanzio, "Homeland Security Takes the Lead in Battle Against Online Child Exploitation: Part Two," NBC10.com, October 8, 2014. www.nbcphiladelphia.com.

52. Quoted in Dane Schiller, "Federal Agents Make Prey of Online Predators Who Search Out Children," *Houston Chronicle*, September 28, 2013. www.houstonchronicle.com.
53. Quoted in Schiller, "Federal Agents Make Prey of Online Predators Who Search Out Children."
54. US Department of Homeland Security, "Stop.Think.Connect.," April 11, 2016. www.dhs.gov.
55. Quoted in CBS Baltimore, "FBI Searching for More Teen Victims of Online Predator," July 8, 2015. http://baltimore.cbslocal.com.
56. Justin W. Patchin, "Most Cyberbullying Cases Aren't Criminal," Cyberbullying Research Center, October 12, 2010. http://cyberbullying.org.
57. Quoted in Mike Masnick, "UK Government Report Recommends Ending Online Anonymity," *Techdirt* (blog), July 30, 2014. www.techdirt.com.
58. Masnick, "UK Government Report Recommends Ending Online Anonymity."
59. Quoted in Alex Fitzpatrick, "Lawmakers Call for an End to Internet Anonymity," Mashable, May 23, 2012. http://mashable.com.
60. Quoted in Lattanzio, "Homeland Security Takes the Lead in Battle Against Online Child Exploitation."
61. Quoted in John Naish, "The NS Profile: Tim Berners-Lee," *New Statesman*, August 15, 2011. www.newstatesman.com.

Enough Is Enough

PO Box 1532
Great Falls, VA 22066
website: www.enough.org
website: www.internetsafety101.org

Enough Is Enough and its Internet safety branch known as Internet Safety 101 is a nonprofit organization that educates, equips, and empowers parents and families to understand and protect themselves from online predators.

Federal Bureau of Investigation

935 Pennsylvania Ave. NW
Washington, DC 20535
phone: (202) 324-3000
website: www.fbi.gov/about-us/investigate/cyber

The FBI is a federal law enforcement agency that investigates and prosecutes online predators through its Cyber Crimes division. The Cyber Crimes division also handles reports of cybercrimes from the public. The FBI website offers information and news about many types of cybercrimes and efforts to combat them.

National Center for Missing & Exploited Children (NCMEC)

Charles B. Wang International Children's Building
699 Prince St.
Alexandria, VA 22314
phone: (800) 843-5678
website: www.missingkids.org

The NCMEC is a government-linked organization that provides information about Internet predators and serves as a clearinghouse for coordinating efforts to track and assist children and teens who are victims of exploitation of any kind.

PACER's National Bullying Prevention Center

2953 Lincoln Blvd.
Santa Monica, CA 90405
phone: (800) 537-2237
website: www.pacer.org/bullying

PACER's National Bullying Prevention Center is a nonprofit organization that provides information and support for anyone concerned about or experiencing bullying. It offers children and teens many ways of becoming involved with preventing and stopping bullying.

Safety Net
phone: (619) 232-2130
website: www.smartcyberchoices.org

Safety Net is a nonprofit organization affiliated with the San Diego Police Department's Internet Crimes Against Children Program. Its website provides information about Internet predators and tips for online safety.

Survivors in Action
website: www.survivorsinaction.org

Survivors in Action is a nonprofit organization dedicated to empowering and helping victims of all types of cyberabuse and cyberbullying. It also advocates for public policies and laws that protect victims of these crimes. Its website offers information and resources for assistance.

US Department of Homeland Security
245 Murray Ln. SW
Washington, DC 20528
phone: (202) 282-8000
website: www.dhs/gov/topic/cybersecurity

The US Department of Homeland Security has several divisions dedicated to protecting the United States and its citizens from cybercrime and tracking and prosecuting cybercriminals. Its website offers information about its anti-cybercrime programs and tips for staying safe online.

FOR FURTHER RESEARCH

Books

Heath Dingwell, *The Truth About the Internet and Online Predators*. New York: Facts On File, 2011.

Stefan Kiesbye, *Cyberpredators*. Farmington Hills, MI: Greenhaven, 2012.

Carla Mooney, *Online Predators*. San Diego: ReferencePoint, 2011.

Patricia D. Netzley, *How Serious a Threat Are Online Predators?* San Diego: ReferencePoint, 2012.

Internet Sources

Stephen Balkam, "Online Safety Redefined: The 3 Key Elements," *Huffington Post*, March 13, 2015. www.huffingtonpost.com/stephen-balkam/online-safety-redefined-t_b_6451870.html.

Tanya Elserer, "How Predators Use Online Games to Lure Children," WFAA ABC News, July 24, 2015. http://legacy.wfaa.com/story/news/crime/2015/07/22/predators-using-online-games-to-lure-children/30549729.

Goodwill Community Foundation, "Internet Safety for Kids: Staying Safe from Online Predators," 2016. www.gcflearnfree.org/internetsafetyforkids/staying-safe-from-online-predators/2.

Chris Hansen, "To Catch a Predator 'III,'" *Dateline NBC*, January 25, 2011. www.nbcnews.com/id/11152602/ns/dateline_nbc/t/catch-predator-iii/#VsP3451.SkS8.

Anna Moore, "I Couldn't Save My Child from Being Killed by an Online Predator," *Guardian* (Manchester, UK), January 23, 2016. www.theguardian.com/lifeandstyle/2016/jan/23/breck-bednar-murder-online-grooming-gaming-lorin-lafave.

Websites

Common Sense Media (www.commonsensemedia.org). Common Sense Media is a nonprofit organization that rates Internet and media products and services with the goal of protecting kids from danger. Its website offers opportunities for kids to learn about how to protect themselves from digital dangers.

Kids Live Safe (www.kidslivesafe.com). The Kids Live Safe website provides extensive information for parents, children, and teens on Internet predators and safety tips in its "Online Predators" section.

NSTeens.org (www.nsteens.org). NSTeens.org is an interactive website sponsored by the National Center for Missing & Exploited Children. It offers teens information, videos, games, and quizzes about online safety.

Safe Internet Surfing (www.safesurfingkids.com). The Safe Internet Surfing website provides information for adults and children about Internet safety. It features quizzes, tips, and information on Internet slang, dangers, and protective software.

StopBullying.gov (www.stopbullying.gov). The StopBullying.gov program strives to educate the public about what cyberbullying is and how to prevent and deal with it. Its website contains information about all aspects of cyberbullying. It also offers support to people affected by bullying.

Teens Against Bullying (www.pacerteensagainstbullying.org). The Teens Against Bullying website was created by and for teens who are dedicated to educating the public and their peers about bullying and ways of fighting it. The Teens Against Bullying program is affiliated with PACER's National Bullying Prevention Center.

INDEX